ADVANCE P\...

THE HIGH SHERIFF OF GREENE

"In this book Claire U. Hertzler has captured the true essence of the man she refers to as 'The High Sheriff of Greene.' Sheriff Wyatt was not just an extremely effective lawman, he was a fine and caring human being whose life and service to all Greene Countians during his long tenure is both memorable and enviable. She tells that story very well."
—Lloyd T. Whitaker, Founder and President of
Newleaf Corporation, Smyrna, GA

"Sheriff L.L. Wyatt served as sheriff of Greene County, GA from 1941-1977. Before becoming sheriff, he was a police officer, cleaning up the moonshine stills in Greene County. He was as tough as nails. In his 36-year career as sheriff, no murder case went unsolved. He would make the "Walking Tall" sheriff look like a choirboy. Wyatt believed in law and order and after his death it took the county twenty years in law and order to get back to normal. I am pleased to see
his story in book form."
—Carey Williams, Editor, The Herald Journal, Greensboro, GA

"To have personally known L.L. Wyatt is something I will always treasure. Known as a legend in the field of law, he was also legendary in other ways. His gentlemanly Southern manner was always at the forefront of whatever he had to do, even when dealing with the most heinous criminal. Wyatt was the likes of what we shall never see again. As his friend and as the Greene County Historian, I am pleased that this work of Claire U. Hertzler will give all the world a chance to know the legendary High Sheriff of Greene."
—W. Joel McCray, Greene County Historian, Greensboro, GA

"This book is a fitting tribute to Sheriff L.L. Wyatt who was the epitome of what a lawman should be. I feel honored to have known him and to have been his daughter-in-law. Claire U. Hertzler has captured well the real 'Wyatt' and told the story in a manner sure to engage the reader from start to finish."
—Madeleine M. Wyatt, daughter-in-law of Sheriff Wyatt

THE HIGH SHERIFF
OF GREENE

THE HIGH SHERIFF
OF GREENE

The True Story of Legendary Lawman L.L. Wyatt

CLAIRE UNDERWOOD HERTZLER

To: Donald,
    Enjoy the read — and
the legend!
        Claire Underwood Hertzler
            11/2016

Published by Deeds Publishing in Athens, GA
www.deedspublishing.com

Cover by Mark Babcock
Layout by Killian Wyatt & Matt King

Printed in The United States of America

Library of Congress Cataloging-in-Publications data is available upon request.

ISBN 978-1-944193-62-1
EISBN 978-1-944193-63-8

Books are available in quantity for promotional or premium use. For information, email info@deedspublishing.com.

First Edition, 2016

10 9 8 7 6 5 4 3 2 1

In recognition of Lloyd Lee "Sonny" Wyatt who gave the book its title and had a long passion to see his father's legacy in print.

This book is dedicated to the memory of my parents, John Garner Underwood, who taught us that a good name is rather to be chosen than great riches, and Gertrude Carter Underwood, who wanted to write a book but, instead, wrote eight, one in the life of each of her children.

Both were admirers of L.L. Wyatt.

Preface

I HAD ALWAYS WANTED, ALWAYS INTENDED TO WRITE A BOOK. MY interest in writing was nourished at an early age by my mother, who dreamed of writing a book herself. Whatever skills I have developed as an author have come about through my experiences in life, in writing news releases, in editing newsletters, in publishing a blog, in digesting the fare of writing workshops/courses, and in hanging out at writers clubs.

One day, I suddenly realized that if I were going to write a book, I had better get going on it. For a year or two, I had considered writing a novel about the cultural clash in my hometown of Greensboro, Georgia, caused by the development of the resorts on Lake Oconee and the subsequent influx of money and talent to a sleepy, rural town.

Before I could get started on the novel, I was sitting with three Atlanta friends in my brother's log cabin in Greene County, listening to his tales of county politics in the years after the loss of long-time policeman and sheriff, L.L. Wyatt. "Claire, there's your book!" one of the friends said. The two others agreed. The stories were compelling, full of local color.

The next day, as I was replaying the Greene County folklore I had heard, the name *L.L. Wyatt* popped into my head again. He was legendary. Had anyone written a book about him? Surely there must be one on such an illustrious figure. A Google search revealed none. I was surprised and energized. I decided to go for it.

Growing up in Greene County during the Wyatt era, I knew who he was. Knew what he looked like. Thought he was handsome. I knew that he tipped his hat to ladies he met on the streets in towns of Greene. But I only knew him from afar until I began writing this book. We were, after all, a law-abiding family and never had occasion to interact personally with "the tall Sheriff of Greene."

Then I remembered a book on my coffee table, *The Greene County, GA, Heritage Book*. Published in 2009 by a heritage committee, the book is a compilation of articles from Greene County history, the past, and present. In it, I found a lengthy article on the life and career of Sheriff Wyatt. And I learned that I was in competition with a Hollywood screenwriter who had spent over a year in Greene County with Wyatt, intending to write a screenplay. I felt strange inserting myself into such a league of writers, but also validated in sensing the drama in Wyatt's life.

Another Google search brought me information about Wyatt's only child, who had retired as a Colonel of the Army and now resided at Reynolds Plantation on Lake Oconee. How convenient to have him near all the other folks I would need to interview.

After some months, I was able to interview Lloyd Lee "Sonny", Wyatt's son, and his wife, Madeleine. Thus began a year and a half dialogue with Sonny and Madeleine, who embraced my efforts wholeheartedly, furnishing information, stories, memorabilia, and contacts. Sonny was in fragile health, which motivated me to stay focused on the completion of the book. However, I did not want to just finish it; I wanted to complete it with integrity and with the honor the Wyatt family deserved.

Unfortunately, after ten months and several surgeries, Sonny's health took a turn from which he was not able to recover. I completed the book with Madeleine's encouragement, hoping that the hours I had spent with Sonny reminiscing about his childhood and his famous father had brought him joy. Sonny was unable to accompany me to any of the local interviews, but I always remembered to tell him just how much his father's legend was still alive and well in the County Greene. Sonny did get to read four completed chapters and give his feedback. He was pleased and happy that Sheriff Wyatt's legacy would soon see print.

I feel blessed to have been the one chosen to do the job. Since Sheriff Wyatt's death, at least two others have begun manuscripts, which were never completed. So, including the screenwriter, I am number four. I have been on a journey of reconnecting with folks in my hometown, re-appreciating my roots, and reliving the Wyatt legacy with many.

I could not have asked for more support from the folks in Greene County and beyond during the birthing of this book. In fact, I would say that this biography was written by the people of Greene County. They think it is about time.

Introduction

OUR CULTURE IS PERPETUALLY LOOKING FOR A HERO, A SOURCE OF inspiration along the journey between good and evil. Someone larger than life to lift us beyond our everyday concerns. This is the story of just such a person. A person like no other, but also very much like us.

"There go Wyatt and Taylor!" we'd shout as Sheriff Wyatt whizzed by in a cloud of dust with his deputy, Willard Taylor. Little did we know that in that cloud of dust rode a hero challenging the norms and changing the behaviors of our county. We did know that *how* those names were said in our household indicated respect akin to awe. And my father did not hand out respect for a public official unless it was merited.

This is the story of a fearless lawman of the deep South, revered by his people, whose life speaks to readers today of courage, honesty, fairness, decency, and utmost respect for the law. This book shows how one man remained determined, from beginning to end, to do the right thing while demanding an unparalleled allegiance to the law. In so doing, Wyatt changed the culture of the entire county.

Folks tested this lawman and found they could not get around him. They found, too, that they could trust him to be a man of his word. These pages paint a picture of a man in public office who operated out of a sense of divine calling and an awareness of God's protection. From this strong inner core, the man came to be known as utterly fearless as he cleaned up the moonshine capital of Georgia and maintained law and order in the County Greene for 52 years.

Doing so required Wyatt to put his own life at risk, resulting in his being "shot at, bitten, threatened, and cursed." One of those times, Wyatt's courage in facing a bank robber catapulted the sheriff into national headlines. This event sealed his status as a legend.

Celestine Sibley once said to a prominent Atlantan whose biography she was about to write, "You know, the story of a good man, leading a good life, ain't necessarily a good book." I felt somewhat the same as I attempted to write this biography. Then, like Sibley, the more details I learned about this man, "the more it seemed to me a good man leading a good life might be the best story of all." This is not a tale of scandal, but rather scintillating tales of daring, of human interest, of the good done, and of crimes prevented.

The book is not an exhaustive biography, but a piecing together of the stories gathered from those who knew L.L. Wyatt personally, from newspaper articles, and from the Wyatt Museum in Greensboro. I have used some creative license to construct dialogue and tie stories together. Most of the words attributed to Wyatt, however, are actual words quoted to me in interviews or cited in newspaper interviews listed under Sources. I have used great care to keep all I have written true to the person and the life I am writing about. Having his own son and his family, as well as the local newspaper editor and others, verify information and validate my depiction has been most helpful in making this a true-to-life account of the life and times of L.L. Wyatt.

I do need to register a disclaimer as to the accuracy of the personal stories told me. I made no attempt to verify them but gladly included them as given, recognizing the fact that they are part of the lore that has kept the legend of Wyatt alive. The stories were told to me by people whose families or friends I have known and whose only motive in the re-telling was to relive the days of their legendary sheriff. And to help a hometown author get it down in print. When requested—or to save embarrassment—I have changed the names of actual persons in the stories.

L.L. Wyatt will become a hero to every reader and inspire them to stand a little taller in the world around them.

1. It Was Moonshine Country Before It Was Bulldog Country

FOUR MEN KICKED THE DOOR OPEN AND STORMED INTO THE room with a strapping, six-foot-one man dripping with blood draped over their shoulders. Five-year-old Sonny watched the men lower his groaning father to the daybed near the living room door. One of the men darted out to call the doctor.

"You really got into a hornet's nest this time," said another of the men as he looked at the gaping holes in the shoulder of the man's black suit.

"Yeah, felt more like the Great War…" the wounded man muttered as he went limp on the bed.

Ol' Doc Adams, known as "Horseshoe Doc," hurried over. The nearest hospital was in Athens, so Doc Adams would have to do. Doc cleaned out the man's gunshot wounds, slapped on a bunch of bandages, and scurried out the door.

Little Sonny ran to his mother, who was now kneeling at her husband's side. "Is Daddy going to be all right? Is he going to die?" Sonny asked, tugging at her skirt.

"No, you know your daddy is strong, and God watches over him," his mom answered, trying to conceal her own fear. Sonny needed her words to reassure him but in his head, he knew the good guy always wins. And L.L. Wyatt was a good man. The fear that could have pervaded the Wyatt household was lessened by a firm trust that God was protecting lawman L.L. Wyatt, the bootlegger's worst enemy in the County Greene.

Some claim that water runs through the Oconee River in the Piedmont area of Georgia, just 30 miles from Athens. But in the earlier part of the 20th century, you could be sure that moonshine coursed through that river as well and in all the creeks in that land. The county was bulging with bootleggers. Greene County was reputed to have the best corn whiskey in Georgia, and it flowed—all the way to the top hotels in Atlanta.

In *The Little Place That Almost Was*, Jan Whyllson wrote, "'Hooch' and 'shine' seemed to be in every part of the forest and high swamp" of Greene County. Rumor was that, in 1920, the then Sheriff of Greene County kept corn whiskey for refreshment in his office in the courthouse. And had a still in his front yard.

But the County Greene had seen better, more reputable days. Between the 1830s and 1850s, the county produced high-quality mercantile products such as buggies, carriages, pistols, and clocks. Orders for these products came from all over the country. The Big Store, still open today on Main Street in Greensboro, served as a superstore, selling "everything from the cradle to the grave." The town's location halfway between Atlanta and Augusta enticed customers from far and wide for a day of shopping and an overnight stay in one of its luxury hotels.

The university's existence in Greenesborough (as it was spelled then) was short-lived. The day after the college opened in August 1787, a band of Creek Indians slipped into town and massacred the women, children, and old men. A few settlers escaped into Fort Greenesborough or the fort at Love Spring. The Indians burned the log courthouse and all twenty cabins. Most of the men and the militia were in Augusta where the new U.S. Constitution was on view, their absence giving the Indians easy access to the town.

Greensboro was the first town in the United States to be burned to the ground and its inhabitants killed by hostile American Indians. The university closed the day after the massacre and was moved up river to friendlier territory. Today, the school is known as the University of Georgia.

In 1833, Mercer University was founded at Penfield in Greene County. But after the Civil War, the founders moved Mercer to Macon, Georgia, to give it a better chance of survival. For a short time, Greensboro also had a Female Academy, where Louisa Mae Alcott was once a teacher. It is still said today that the locals were pleased to have these institutions moved, as "the boys would steal their apples" and "the girls giggled too much."

Fifty years after its founding, in the 1830s, Greene County became the largest cotton producing county in Georgia. Cotton was hailed as king in Greene County, and its reign saw a proliferation of stores, banks, and civic buildings in Greensboro.

By the arrival of the Civil War, King Cotton had exhausted the productivity of the land in this rich cotton belt. Even so, after the war, the county soon returned its allegiance to cotton. With the demise of the plantation system in Greene, a market economy resulted in which tenant farmers or owners of small farms were at the bottom, and merchants and lawyers were at the top.

Then, in 1915, the King's dreaded enemy, the boll weevil, invaded Georgia. Greene County believed its cotton to be "weevil-proof", but by 1922, the enemy had decimated cotton production, even in the County Greene. The boom time in Greensboro ended.

The devastation of the cotton industry, together with the passage of national Prohibition in 1919, created the impetus for folks to turn to moonshining, some for survival and others for greed. The Prohibition law, though it yielded some intended good effects, fueled an illegal liquor industry, an industry that thrived in the County Greene.

In 1920, organized bootlegging began to surface throughout the country as National Prohibition went into effect. The moonshiner who had survived as a craftsman in small towns, such as many in Georgia, was quickly replaced by gangsters. A black market for the alcohol grew rapidly and turned violent. In larger cities, police department costs rose significantly because of "black market violence."

It was no: illegal to possess or to consume whiskey privately; it was illegal to manufacture, transport, or sell the whiskey. The Internal Revenue Service was given the job of enforcing Prohibition. After two years, enforcement was handed over to the Justice Department. The advocates of Prohibition had no idea that it would be almost impossible to enforce.

The refreshing gourmet taste of Greene County's moonshine was the beverage of choice in Atlanta's finest hotels. The County Greene gained the distinction of becoming the moonshine capital of Georgia and for some, the country. That reputation was a recognition of both the Wild West atmosphere that fed the industry and the sought-after taste.

Law enforcement went after the makers and haulers of moonshine like bird dogs teasing out their prey. The enforcement agents sent from the IRS were called "feds" or revenuers. The bootleggers revamped their vehicles to outrun these "revenooers." Rick Houston in an article on NASCAR.com wrote, "They souped up their cars to haul bounty, and then ran from the law like their behinds were on fire." From these chases, made famous by local yarns, came the NASCAR races of today. Rick Houston wrote further, "NASCAR's roots are soaked to the very tips in moonshine." Bootleggers arranged the loads for the "moonshine runners" or haulers who most often made their runs in the light of the moon.

A dangerous game of cat and mouse developed in which the revenuer and the moonshiner attempted to outwit, outrun and outlive the other. The bootlegger and their lookouts set up elaborate systems to warn the still of the approaching "feds." Neighbors or persons stationed near the still and paid to watch and warn would set off a signal. The signal would travel from lookout to lookout until the message reached the still.

Everything felt corrupted during Prohibition, quite the opposite of the intended goal to clean up the morals of the country. No one knew who to trust or who was in the pockets of the moonshine business. Most regarded even their neighbor with suspicion during Prohibition, believing every man had his price. The Greensboro *Herald Journal* commented, "It is nauseating to the average man when he learns just how much damnable rottenness there is in the would-be Prohibition forces all over America." The honest law enforcement agents, sheriffs, and police officers often found their lives at risk.

It was into this turf-war of corruption that the Board of Commissioners of the County Greene sought to bring some law and order in the year 1925. Their hopes hung on the fresh honesty of rookie lawman L.L. Wyatt. The same Wyatt who by 1927 would become the bootlegger's worst enemy—and his biggest target.

One of the Oldest Operational Courthouses in Georgia

2. The Best Set of Legs in Georgia

"I KNOW A BOY BACK IN PAULDING COUNTY WE MIGHT GET," SAID the Rev. Robert Stewart, pastor of the Greensboro United Methodist Church, to Commissioner Henry Spinks. The Commission was fed up with the ineffectiveness of its two policemen. "This farm boy has been working with his uncle who's a deputy. This young fella' can outrun any bootlegger in the county. And he's as honest as the day is long."

A few days later, policemen Sturdivant and Lovejoy resigned.

"Well," Spinks said to Rev. Stewart, "let's get that boy you were talking about down here for a look."

On Monday, three days later, the "boy" drove up in a weathered Ford. He was now 21 years old. He unfolded himself from the car and placed his feet on Main Street in front of the courthouse. The men fixed on the bench by the sidewalk looked him over from toe to head.

"Look at them legs," one man said as he spat his tobacco juice onto the sidewalk.

"Who is he anyway?" asked another.

"Maybe he's in trouble with the law," ventured a third as the men watched the stranger walk toward the door of the courthouse.

"He don't look like a criminal," the first man said, "but it's for sure he ain't from around here."

The young man pushed open the twelve-foot tall, carved oak doors of the 1849 vintage courthouse. He looked around for someone to direct him and ran smack into Sheriff Hixon, who was hurrying out. The sheriff, unaware of what was about to transpire, pointed to the conference room where the commissioners had already gathered. The young man knocked on the door.

"Well, greetings, Mr. Wyatt," the chairman said as he extended a handshake. "I'm Henry Spinks. Glad to meet you. We appreciate your coming down."

"Glad to be here," the visitor replied.

The chairman introduced Loy Lee Wyatt to the men seated at the table and then motioned him to a seat.

"Just call me Wyatt," Wyatt said as he sat down.

"All right, Wyatt, we want to welcome you to the moonshine capital of Georgia, and some say the nation! We are not proud of this reputation. We know our folks have to make a living somehow. But the stuff is illegal and creates black market crime. Our county is being shredded by the guns and corrupted by the payoffs that go on. Even the respectable families are not immune. Some of them are imbibing the stuff and raking money off the top of the industry. We used to have a decent community. We were a desirable place to live and do business. But here of late, we've become a lawless jungle."

The commissioner paused a moment and studied the face of the young man sitting there. Wyatt looked at Spinks and nodded his head to let him know he got the picture.

"Sounds a lot like Paulding," said Wyatt.

"No, it's not like Paulding," piped up Commissioner L.P. Whelchel, who had heard about Paulding from his pastor, the Rev. Stewart. "Greene has more moonshiners per square mile than *any* county in Georgia."

Henry Spinks continued, "That's why we need you here. We have to have a police officer who is not afraid to tackle this problem. Who *can* and *will* go after these folks and clean up our county. The police officers who just resigned were doing next to nothing. I'm glad they're gone. We are right certain they were being bribed to look the other way.

They closed some stills last year but arrested only six folks. And our sheriff—well, he likes it the way it is, what with a still in his own yard."

"Yeah, you have to know Hixon believes every man has a God-given right to drink as he wills. So don't count on his covering you," Commissioner R.E. Stapleton added. "We can give you names of operators and approximate locations of stills right now. The ones who 'own' the county are well known. We just need somebody who knows how to go after them."

Stapleton continued, "You know, moonshining is a complex issue. You hate to take away the only means of income some folks have. They need a way to survive. Some of them are women who are trying to support a house full of children. Then you have the part-timers who are supplementing a less than adequate income. But the worst of all, and the most vicious, are those who have made it an industry, like over in Carey's Station. And when you are a county policeman, you are making arrests of folks you have to live with or beside. Sometimes you go to church with them. It takes good judgment."

"We will take you out in the county and point out some of the sites later. Maybe we can drive over to Carey's Station, too," Whelchel said.

"Well," replied Wyatt, "I'm of age now, so I hope I have good judgment most of the time anyway. Reverend Stewart can vouch for my maturity and my skills in the woods."

Chairman Spinks steered the conversation back to the would-be bootleg fighter. "You do come highly recommended by the Reverend Stewart, but why don't you tell us about yourself and your experience? You're awfully young, but we understand that you have worked some with an uncle who is a deputy up in Paulding County."

"Well, my uncle, he's a good teacher. He and my daddy formed a Law and Order Vigilante League up there in the Beulahland community. Mostly it was folks from Beulahland Baptist Church where we go. But Reverend Stewart was a regular, too. We called him the 'Raiding

Parson' since he seemed totally committed to the cause. We go out once a month to locate the stills and tear them down. I guess y'all already know that the Rev's wife was killed by a moonshiner's bullet intended for the parson. It was a sad thing, but we kept the raids going as she would have wanted.

"Uncle J.W. needed me to do the running and catching of the bootleggers. So he deputized me when I was seventeen. He has had me going in with him to break up the stills. We've done a good number of them; he showed me how to stake them out, how to know when to go in after the bootleggers," Wyatt continued.

"And when to run 'em down?" one of the men asked.

"Yeah, that's the fun part," answered Wyatt.

"Tell us more about your family. What else have you been doing since you got out of school?" Whelchel asked.

"Well," Wyatt said, "I am number three in a family of eight. We worked hard all our lives on the farm, just barely making it. I been building cabinets and doing carpentry when I wasn't helping my uncle. My daddy is Justice of the Peace, and he deputized me when I was thirteen. He had me goin' out there to help scout out the stills before I actually started chasing down the bootleggers at seventeen."

"My goodness, I don't know whether to call that courageous or crazy! Questions anyone?" the chairman asked.

"Yes, sir," Wyatt answered. "How many stills would you say are in the county?"

"Hundreds," came a loud chorus from the commissioners.

"That sounds like some good daily bread for me," Wyatt said with a chuckle. "Do I get to do this single-handedly?"

"Well, we have hired another policeman to work with you; even with your reputation, you'll need some backup. He knows the county, but he is in his mid-fifties, so he'll need some younger legs to chase 'em down," answered Henry Spinks.

"Now, if we are able to work something out with you, you can rent a room from the person we're hiring, T. Griff Williams," Stapleton volunteered, "they have a large house, and you could get your meals there, too."

Spinks pulled out his pocket watch and announced, "Speaking of meals, gentlemen, I think it's about time for a lunch break."

The men walked down to the intersection of Main and Broad and entered Armor Hunter Drug Store. They chose one of the three tables in the 67-year-old building. Their corner table allowed them to watch the U.S. 278/Broad Street traffic going through town and the locals walking to lunch down Main Street.

Rev. Stewart joined the group, giving Wyatt a hearty embrace and a welcoming handshake. Wyatt was pleased to see the "Raiding Parson", who had sensed there might be a divinely appointed lawman in young Wyatt. Rev. Stewart had felt God's hand on Wyatt as he prayed protection over him before he went out on his first raid.

Melinda, the waitress, eyed Wyatt as she walked over. She liked what she saw, especially when Wyatt got up halfway out of his chair, extended his hand and said, "Hello, Melinda."

He sat back down as she asked, "You new around here? And you're hanging around with these folks?" She laughed as she pointed to the rest of the group. "Where did y'all find such a handsome young thing?"

Not wanting to reveal who their guest was, Spinks said, "We're just showing him around the town. And we're ready for some of your good food."

"What'll you have?"

Wyatt ordered a BLT with sweetened iced-tea and a piece of lemon meringue pie. The four other men placed similar orders, except for one hamburger. When the tea arrived, Whelchel raised his glass and said, "Armor Hunter has the best iced-tea anywhere around. And it isn't even laced with anything." The others lifted their glasses as they let out knowing laughter.

"The County Greene has a population of 18,972 persons, and sometimes I think about half of them are moonshiners!" Stapleton said.

"Well, we'll cut that down to size in no time," said Wyatt and then, pointing to the windows, he continued, "You know, as a cabinet maker, I just can't take my eyes off these heart-of-pine walls and window trim. When was this place built?"

"It was constructed in 1858," Spinks said, "and it *is* beautiful. Over there diagonally across is Chandler's Drug Store, formerly the luxury Statham Hotel. Inside that store, Chandler served the first Coca-Cola in Greene County. Too bad Coca-Cola didn't put a damper on the taste for moonshine. But I think I did read that the Coke stocks have been going up during Prohibition.

"Across Broad here, up on the top floor, is *The Herald Journal* run by J.C. Williams. He's been at it for about ten years. I imagine his son, Carey, will inherit the paper someday if he wants it. It's the county's weekly news and voice."

Satisfied with food, the men walked across Broad to J.H. McCommons's The Big Store. "We want you to see the McCommons Funeral Company here above The Big Store. I expect McCommons will succeed the current county coroner some day. They are trustworthy folks and have been here a long time. The McCommons family has had The Big Store since 1900," Whelchel said, pointing to The Big Store sign.

"Well, that's a brief tour. We need to head out if we're going to show you the rural parts," said Spinks.

They walked back up Main, past Weinstein's Dry Goods, Goldstein's Variety Store, The Ten Cents Store, Mrs. Geer's Café, and across the street to the courthouse. The chairman opened the door to his black Model T Ford, which was parked in front of the courthouse. Wyatt smiled. "I like Fords, too," he said.

The men drove Wyatt out to the Greshamville area, along Lingerlonger Creek, and to the dirt road near Jernigan's Bridge. They drove back past timber land near Flat Rock and to Walker's Church Road, pointing out where there might be stills. They said they were not certain where the stills were; they had only *heard* things. Except for Carey's Station, which everybody knew about.

As they were riding along Lingerlonger Creek, Henry Spinks handed Wyatt a map of the County Greene and said, "See how the county is a thin area following the Oconee River from Flat Shoals, up the Apalachee River north to High Shoals? I've outlined it with a red pencil. Greene covers 374 square miles, an area 22 miles long and 17 miles wide. And all that territory is as thick with bootleggers as the pine trees that hide them. That would be your happy hunting ground.

"Actually, the land over by the Oconee was the hunting grounds of the Creek Indians for over 10,000 years. Land grabbers with questionable permits from the state started taking that land, and that's when the Indians came into Greensboro and burned it to the ground. Now, we need another kind of hunter."

When they told him he was on Lingerlonger Creek, Wyatt rolled down the window, announcing, "I just want to get a whiff of all that mash you say is on this creek!" He charmed the men with tales about the Law and Order Vigilante League and the unloaded gun he carried to intimidate the bootleggers.

"Man, y'all should have seen the looks we got when we rode them first two bootleggers and their still through the streets up there in Rockmart," Wyatt said. "Let me tell you; when you catch that first one, it gets the attention of the rest. Especially if that one has always outrun the law before!"

The commissioners were in awe, and Whelchel joked, "Heck, can you start tonight?" They continued to give Wyatt an earful of what he would face in Greene County as they drove over to Carey's Station.

"There are enough stills along Lingerlonger Creek and Carey's Station to keep all the hotels in Atlanta and beyond supplied, I'll wager,"

Stapleton said as they neared Carey's Station. "There's so much traffic over here at Carey's Station, it's called 'Little New York.' About fifty cars a day come through here, leaving with loads for all the major cities in Georgia. I hear there are at least a dozen stills operating over here. The industry is so large some of the stills have three shifts of workers. They'll be after you for sure and with big money, too." Wyatt smiled at the thought of someone's attempting to bribe him.

At half past three p.m., they drove back and parked the Model T next to Wyatt's Ford at the courthouse. "Well, what do you think so far?" Spinks asked.

"I know I can handle the job," said a confident Wyatt. "If I take it, I will give it my best shot. Well, maybe I shouldn't use *that* word," Wyatt said with a laugh, "because I hope I don't have to shoot, but I *am* a pretty good shooter. I believe in the law, but I also believe in respecting peoples' lives. Vigilante without violence is how I've been doing it."

"Well, there's one other person we need you to meet. Willard Taylor has led the citizen charge against the moonshine industry, and his enemies set his house afire. When the fire department got there, they chopped up the hoses. We told you our county is a moonshine wilderness. What they did to Taylor, they'll do to you, or worse. We just need him to meet you and be behind what we do. Can you meet him and Stapleton in Atlanta at the Henry Grady Hotel on Thursday, Room 606?" asked Chairman Spinks.

"I'll be there," said Wyatt, "and I'll try to make a believer out of him."

On Thursday in Room 606, things didn't start out too well in the secret face-to-face meeting Stapleton had arranged. After introductions had been made, Taylor stepped back to get a good look at young Wyatt. He didn't seem too impressed.

Looking at the innocent young fellow, Taylor got serious. "Now, son, I have to be honest with you. I don't see how you and Williams can get the job done. It's like one is too young and the other too old. No offense to either of you, but we're talking about one of the biggest bootleg operations in the country," Taylor said with exasperation.

Wyatt said respectfully, "Just give us a chance, Mr. Taylor. Mr. Williams knows where all the stills are, and I know how to catch 'em. If I could do it in Paulding, I can do it in Greene." Wyatt had no idea the sparks he had just set off.

Taylor's face grew red. "I will tell you one thing, there is no county in Georgia or anywhere else that can be compared to Greene County when it comes to bootlegging. And you better hear what I'm saying."

Wyatt sat attentively as Taylor launched into his version of what was going on in Greene. Wyatt was intrigued to hear Taylor's description of the vastness of the moonshine industry at Carey's Station. Until a few days ago, he had never seen an operation big enough to have fifty cars a day hauling moonshine to cities all over Georgia and beyond. Wyatt couldn't wait to meet the owners and their crowd, despite Taylor's dire predictions of the lengths these folks would go to sabotage a young, honest lawman.

"Mr. Taylor, I'll take my chances. You see, I do a lot of praying on the job," Wyatt responded with an air of fearlessness.

Taylor, looking curiously at Wyatt, suggested they head to the coffee shop to talk further. On the elevator, Taylor was privy to Wyatt's interaction with the elevator-operator.

"Do you think they'll ever bust up that Greene County bootlegging you were telling me about on the way up? Before I can get some of that corn whiskey?" asked Wyatt.

"Ain't nobody gonna' bust that up. 'Cause they's getting paid off. And nobody's gettin' caught," answered the operator, wondering why this fellow was so interested but not asking for a taste.

"What kind of experience would it take to catch somebody down there?" asked Wyatt, keeping the bantering going for Taylor's sake.

"Don't take none. All it'd take is some fast feet to flat run 'em down."

"Thank you," Wyatt said as the elevator reached the lobby.

In the lobby, Taylor, now more hopeful, told Stapleton to have Wyatt report on Monday morning.

The commissioners offered Wyatt the job that day...Wyatt took it for $200 a month.

3. Watering the Ground with Mash

LOY LEE WYATT ARRIVED FOR DUTY HIS FIRST DAY IN A BLACK SUIT, white shirt with black tie, and a black wide-brimmed Stetson hat. This outfit became his signature dress for the next 52 years on the job. On the lapel of his black suit, he wore a police badge about the size of a quarter, which he had ordered from a police officers mail order catalog.

In the courthouse, Wyatt raised his right hand and solemnly swore the Oath of Office of Police. Though he did not say so directly, Wyatt was vowing to take on the illegal liquor industry and to clean up the County Greene.

Then Wyatt went out to do his job. The first day, October 13, 1925, five years into Prohibition, Wyatt and T. Griff Williams, hired at the same time, got a head start. They drove the back roads and scouted out some stills. Williams, now Wyatt's landlord, was born and bred in Greene County, so he knew the roads and the rumors. And Wyatt knew about chasing down the bootleggers.

They walked through the woods toward a still, watching the movement of every tree and every bush and listening for any unnatural sound. As they neared the still, they dropped to the ground and crawled through the brush, inching nearer and nearer to the smell of the mash. When they were confident of their advantage, they moved as silently as death to the still. They chopped it up and unplugged the vats, allowing thousands of dollars worth of mash to rush to the ground. They moved on to another and shut it down.

"Can you believe this?" Wyatt asked his partner. "Let's keep going and see how many we can do this first day–okay?" Out there on the edge, the excitement was almost addictive. Once the adrenaline got going, the two felt invincible. To Wyatt, it seemed somehow like a calling. A calling from God to fight this evil. At the end of the first day, they had shut down six stills, pouring out tens of thousands of gallons of distilled mash. There were going to be some unhappy folks in the County Greene tonight! Wyatt said to a newspaper reporter, "The first sixty days, Williams and I found and destroyed 62 large stills. We got six big ones the first day. I mean they had 12 to 15 vats holding 500 gallons of mash apiece."

A whopping total of 45,000 gallons of Greene County's famous corn whiskey poured out on the ground the first day! At the top rate in 1925 of $1.00 a gallon, that's a steep loss of $500 a vat, or a total of $45,000; in 2015 prices, the loss would be $2,925,000 at an average price of $65 a gallon.

With this price tag, moonshining was a better return on the dollar than almost anything a man or woman could do to feed their family, particularly those on the bottom of the economic ladder. For others, moonshining was an industry so large it required three shifts of workers. It not only paid the workers, it also paid off any and everyone the owners needed to silence to protect their golden mash.

The possibility of a large pay-off did nothing to deter Wyatt. In 1926, he and Williams rode through town with the workings of a copper still wrapped around the car for all to see. It was one of 126 stills they captured that first year; the copper components were the primary reason Greene County's corn liquor boasted such a superior taste.

On another occasion, they brought into town a ton and a half truck loaded with 50–100 gallons of moonshine. As they emptied the jugs on the courthouse lawn, folks gathered around, holding their hands out for the free 'shine!' Not a few wanted to cry as the good stuff seeped into the ground under their feet. *What a waste!*

Wyatt's moonshine cleanup did not always happen out in the woods.

Stories abounded of people's encounters with Wyatt during his cleanup campaign. He cultivated "lookouts" all over the county, at least one in each of the ten districts. Some folks wondered if the informants got special favors in exchange for the information. However, Wyatt was not heartless. He would give folks a chance first. If he got a tip that someone was selling illegal liquor, Wyatt would go to that person and say, "You know, I had a dream last night that you were selling whiskey. If you are, please stop. If you are not selling whiskey, disregard this dream."

Wyatt, as one story has it, went to the home of a woman and said, "How are you, Daisy? How're you feeling? Daisy, I see some smoke down behind your house. Looks like it's down by the path there. You know, if I see that smoke again, I'm gonna' have to go down that path and see what that fire is all about."

"That man Wyatt hadn't left my property good before I was out there destroying that still," Daisy said, explaining how she lost her business. "I knew that he knew; he was just giving me some time." It wasn't his words; it was the *I'm doing you a favor, but I will enforce the law* look that got folks' attention.

In October 1926, Wyatt and Williams were nearing the end of their first year as county police officers. They had just made a bust of yet another large still and captured the two still workers. This was celebrated with a termination notice, effective November 1, for both of them. Henry Spinks was apologetic as he explained, "I'm sorry, but some of the commissioners have complained about your work." They were dismissed without any charges or any chance to defend themselves. Wyatt and Williams guessed that the "moonshine mafia" had enticed or threatened the commissioners. Since the commissioners were leaving office in two months, they caved, seeing they had little to lose.

Sheriff E.C. Hixson—the sheriff who kept moonshine in his office—took over the job at $200 a month. Greensboro's *Herald Journal* and a delegation of women devotees protested the dismissal of Williams and

Wyatt and demanded their reinstatement. The women were keenly aware of how moonshine was destroying families and communities. Wyatt had captivated the women's allegiance, too, with his habit of tipping his hat in respect each time he met a lady on the street. Though gentlemen customarily tipped their hats to women at the time, a tall policeman doing so made a memorable impression.

Wyatt stayed in the county and worked as a hired gun for a federal revenuer, K. M. Brock, who was known as "The Black Spider", and covered eight counties. Wyatt earned a fee of $9.00 for each moonshiner he caught if those he apprehended were prosecuted. He became a sort of bounty-hunter for the area.

On February 1, 1927, the new Board of Commissioners reinstated L.L. Wyatt as a county police officer and hired J. Edward Clifton as a new policeman. The new Board consisted of Henry D. Goodwin, Chair, Harold Lamb, and Dr. C. C. King. The salary of the police officers was reduced to $150 each per month.

T. Griff Williams was named security guard at Mary-Leila Cotton Mills, one of the largest employers in the county. In later years, Williams and Wyatt would work together again when Sheriff Wyatt named Williams his bailiff. Williams served as bailiff through his late nineties. He walked everywhere and never took medicine, not even an aspirin. Wyatt, who came to be known for his stamina, must have received a few tips on endurance from T. Griff Williams.

After a close call in a shootout at a still, Clifton resigned as Wyatt's partner. Wyatt worked alone for almost a year, trying out several partners, all of whom found the work too tough. Finally, Willard Taylor who had once doubted Wyatt's capacity for the job, signed on as his partner. "Wyatt and Taylor" became a familiar sight and a household reference in Greene County as the two worked together effectively for years to come.

Watering the Ground was a Frequent Happening with Wyatt

4. Taking Wyatt Out

WYATT BEGAN A COURTSHIP WITH ESTELLE BRASWELL, WHO WAS from Draketown, Georgia, near Rockmart. They were married in 1928. Wyatt took his bride over the threshold to their living quarters in the home of T. Griff Williams. The imposing gingerbread house sat on a hill overlooking Greensboro.

Estelle was a woman of vibrant energy, and she had a beautiful face framed with soft curls. The Wyatts had a quiet, loving relationship. Estelle supported her husband one hundred percent, transporting Wyatt to possible stills, delivering prisoners to their cells, and cooking meals for the incarcerated.

Estelle often "took Wyatt out," as she called it, to drop him on a desolate back road so he could sneak through the woods to the stills. She picked him up an hour later. The strategy worked. No one expected a woman driver to be out looking for the moonshiners, certainly not at night. Estelle, using disguises and borrowed cars, continued taking Wyatt out over the years, even to nearby counties.

Their only child, Lloyd Lee "Sonny," was born on March 11, 1931. To Wyatt, a day's work was being on call twenty-four hours; to Estelle and Sonny, it was facing daily questions. Would Wyatt come home tonight? When would he come home? Would he come home alive?

From the Williams's home, Wyatt and Estelle moved with Sonny into the upstairs apartment in the house of J.W. Hunter, Chief of Police. Later, they purchased their first house on Walnut Street, where Estelle enjoyed having a place of her own.

Estelle, who liked culinary pursuits, was disappointed to find that food meant little to Wyatt. Though he appreciated the meals she prepared, Wyatt is quoted by fellow lawman Hilyer Tuggle as saying, "I eat when I don't have anything else to do."

Though Estelle had a quiet personality, she gained a reputation as a loving, kind, and generous person throughout the community. The Wyatt's home served as a food pantry for folks who needed help. Terry Randall told how his mother's family survived for a time on bags of meal and other staples Estelle brought them each month.

Estelle became active in the community as a founding member of the Greensboro Garden Club, in the life of the Greensboro Baptist Church, and as president of the Women's Christian Temperance Union, an office she held for 20 years. This group made a fitting ally to Wyatt, never failing to pass along their strategies for closing in on a bootlegger.

Miss Estelle

Estelle with baby Sonny

Sonny at three years

Wyatt with Sonny

Wyatt with 10 year old Sonny

5. "Shot At, Bitten, and Cursed"

WYATT WAS RE-HIRED IN 1927, AND THOSE WHO PREVIOUSLY HAD free reign in Greene's Wild West moonshine wilderness didn't like what they saw in this new police officer. They had to put a stop to him before he put a stop to them. They started with, literally, a dynamite plan.

Wyatt gave his account of these tactics in several different newspaper interviews. As he recalled, his enemies began by leaving six sticks of dynamite on his front porch. Wyatt picked up the explosives and found a note attached: "Stay out of the woods." *I guess I'm getting through to somebody,* he must have thought.

When the moonshiners saw Wyatt meant business, things got meaner. The dynamite didn't stop him, so they tried something else: they poured shellac into the engine of his car. "That set me back financially as policemen had to buy their own cars," Wyatt said to reporter Prentice Palmer, "but it didn't stop me."

"The next thing they tried was making me an offer," Wyatt continued, "an offer of a $1,000 a month if I let them operate and told me if it worked out, they would give me a raise!" For a police officer making $150 a month and furnishing his own car, that money would have been hard to resist. L.L. Wyatt did not fall into the trap.

His enemies were desperate. Next, they pulled out their guns. In 1927, three years into the job, Wyatt took fire during four different incidents in a three-month period. "Most of them were flesh wounds," Wyatt said, "but I got shot at again three times in 1933. I was off the job for six months. One of the bullets smashed my kneecap."

These wounds were inflicted one cold February night at the railroad trestle bridge at Carey's Station. Wyatt and Taylor were waiting for loggers who were stealing logs and floating them down the Oconee River. Up on the trestle bridge walked two moonshiners coming into Greene County with sacks of moonshine over their shoulders. Wyatt shouted to the first rumrunner, "Stop! You're under arrest."

The rumrunner pulled out his .45 automatic and aimed at Wyatt's chest. What he hit was Wyatt's left leg above the knee. The second shot hit Wyatt's right leg, and as Wyatt was struggling to get his gun from the holster under his overcoat, a third shot split his kneecap. Willard Taylor, Wyatt's deputy, aimed his weapon and killed the bootlegger. The other bootlegger ran back across the trestle and into the night.

Taylor managed to get Wyatt to his car and to Doc Adams, who cleaned out the wounds. The bullets had not lodged in the leg or knee, so Doc wrapped on some bandages and sent Wyatt home. A week later, the knee became infected, and Estelle took Wyatt to St. Mary's Hospital in Athens. Once the infection seemed under control, he was dismissed.

The knee began to stiffen, and there was a question as to whether Wyatt would be able to walk again. The bootleggers took heart and went to their work with new vigor.

Wyatt then became a patient at Emory Rehabilitation Center for six weeks. Within six months, and to the surprise of the bootleggers, he walked out the door of his home without even a limp.

Though Wyatt did not usually carry a gun on his person, having to always go to the car for his weapon, he did shoot some folks. In his cleanup of the county, Wyatt killed at least six men, all of whom shot at him first. Some say he killed as many as nine. He didn't like to remember those incidents. Of one, Wyatt told a reporter, "I wish there had been another way."

This particular shooting happened in 1927 when Wyatt and three other officers went to search the property of John Neal, a person suspected of bootlegging. Wyatt told the suspect what the officers were doing and asked for access to search the house.

"Okay, Mr. Wyatt, let me go find the key," said Neal.

A neighbor produced a key, and two officers went into the house, followed by Neal. Chief of Police J.H. Jones and Wyatt were searching the outside premises. They asked Wyatt to go to the front to catch Neal if he tried to run while Jones entered through the back door.

Neal had secured an automatic shotgun by this time and began shooting. According to Wyatt, "My partner went down. The two remaining officers were hit before one of us managed to shoot the shotgun out of his hand." Neal was shot twice in the chest during the exchange of fire but managed to escape to a nearby house where he barricaded himself.

When Wyatt knocked on the door, a lady spoke through the closed door, saying, "There's someone sick in here, and I can't open the door."

Wyatt kicked the door in and found a shotgun at point blank range in his face. Neal pulled the trigger, but the gun did not fire. "The only reason he didn't shoot me was his shotgun jammed," said Wyatt. "He had me cold when I came through the door."

Wyatt continued, "I took the chief and the deputies to the hospital and headed for the county jail with the suspect passed out in the back seat." Unexpectedly, the suspect came to, grabbed Wyatt's gun from the front seat, and began beating Wyatt over the head.

Describing the scene to a reporter, Wyatt said, "I went over the seat of the car–it was an old touring car–and we started fighting. He got my left ear in his mouth, and I couldn't get it loose. I finally got a finger in his mouth and pried his jaws apart."

The car was driving itself down the hill on Court Street, as if it knew its own way to the jail. G.W. Miles saw the driverless car, jumped onto the running board, and grasped the gun, intending to shoot the suspect. Miles discovered that the weapon was empty, so he began to hit the suspect on the head with the gun. The suspect, to ward off the blow, released his hold on Wyatt. Miles jumped off the running board. Wyatt felt for his ear, which was miraculously still there.

According to Wyatt, "The car chugged to a stop." The suspect fell out of the car, and Wyatt shot him. It is said that Wyatt wore the brand of that moonshiner's teeth for the rest of his life.

It was in 1936 when the four men stormed into Wyatt's home with the "moonshiner's worst enemy in the county Greene" on their shoulders. The blood dripping from their victim was coming from wounds made by a load of buckshot he had taken in the shoulder during a house raid. Ol' Doc Adams came to the rescue by removing the pellets, swabbing out the wounds with iodine, and slapping on a bunch of bandages.

Wyatt's worst injuries occurred just as the mood of the country was turning toward the repeal of Prohibition. The national Prohibition Law was repealed in 1933, then Georgia's Prohibition Law in 1935. Counties in Georgia were allowed to continue their "dry" status, which the County Greene maintained until 1982. Wyatt still had work to do.

One evening, Wyatt waited at the Greenland Theater for a rumrunner to arrive. One of his informants had sent word that a white moonshiner in Hancock County was paying a black man to drive his moonshine into Greene County.

Transactions were made right on Main Street at the only theater in town. The rumrunner was checking things out as he pulled into the parking lot.

"Darned if that isn't that L.L. Wyatt," he muttered, wondering what to do.

Wyatt walked over to him, stared him in the eye, and said, "I know you brought a load of moonshine here tonight, and if you ever come back to Greene County, I will throw you in jail!" He was never seen in Greene again.

In a similar incident, recorded in the book, *Do Tell*, Wyatt gave another moonshine peddler one of his famous warnings. A few weeks later,

Wyatt told the same man, "Tom, on your bootleg run last night, you walked so close to me, I could have touched you. I was hidin' in the bushes watching for Greene County folks." Hiding in the bushes for moonshiners was old hat for Wyatt.

In court, though, Wyatt would look for a way to help folks, "Judge, that fellow over there is mean, bad to the bone. But this is a pretty good ole boy here; he just got mixed up with the wrong crowd."

For 15 years, at the height of prohibition, Wyatt served as a policeman for the County Greene. He established himself as fearless, honest, and tireless. He never, ever compromised his principles. The word on the back roads and the streets was, "You don't fool with that Wyatt fellow; he's gonna' do what's right so you better do the same!"

Spurgion Cayler once worked the large stills and at 79 years of age, he told a newspaper of his days with Wyatt, "Back in those days people were making $3.00 a week on a regular job. I was getting $20.00 a week for making liquor for a white boss. If caught they agreed to pay the fine and if there was a jail sentence they would pay your salary while in jail. I wasn't proud of the work I was doing but the pay kept me from starving.

"When Mr. L.L. Wyatt started raiding the stills I thought he would get killed, but he wasn't scared. Once he ran me for three miles in the swamps. I got six months jail sentence. When I got out of jail the moonshine business was dead here and I never went back to that kind of work."

Wyatt cleared the county of moonshiners almost entirely in his first five years.

Giant Moonshine Still Raided, 6. Arrested In Large Liquor Operation

OVER $28,000 OF MOONSHINE CONFISCATED

One of the largest moonshine whiskey stills in the history of Greene County was raided early Friday morning July 30th.

The still was located, 9 miles from Greensboro, 2 miles off Georgia highway 44 known as the Eatonton-Greensboro highway.

A team of county, state and federal agents raided the large still and seized more than 2,830 gallons of illegal liquor.

The moonshine seized was valued at more than $28,000 on the whiskey market.

The still, an upright boiler type, was said to have a 9,000 gallon capacity and the capacity to turn out 800 gallons of whiskey a day. Officers said they confiscated 824 gallons of whiskey in one gallon jugs at the still site.

2,300 gallons of moonshine was found at a home in Morgan County. Officers stated that the 2,000 gallons of moonshine came from the Greene County whiskey still.

The officers did not speculate on how long the distillery may have been in operation, but described it as "a dandy". It was a giant.

Greene County Sheriff L. L. Wyatt told the Herald Journal that five men were arrested near the whiskey still and another in a house in Morgan County where 2,000 gallons of the moonshine was found.

Charged with manufacturing and possessing non-tax paid liquor were John I. "Buddy" Richardson, 45, of Madison, Eugene Perry, 34, of Dahlonega, M. C. Perry, 32, of Cleveland, Dutch Denard, 36, of Dawsonville and John Moses Green, 34, of Greensboro.

Leonard Mapp of Madison was arrested on possession charges when officers found the moonshine stashed in his house near Madison. Sheriff Wyatt stated, 2,000 gallons of moonshine in one gallon jugs were found at the Mapp house.

The still and the whiskey were destroyed Friday afternoon. Officers used dynamite in destroying the huge still and the large quantity of illegal whiskey.

The six men were arraigned Monday before U. S. officials in Macon.

MOONSHINE MAKERS DON'T DRINK THEIR OWN STUFF

"Moonshine is to be sold, not to drink by the maker," is the words of Eugene Perry who was caught Friday at a large still in Greene County. Over 800 gallons of moonshine in one gallon jugs were ready to go on the market. The workers drank government whiskey. A near empty bottle of blended whiskey that the workers sipped on was on a table near the large still.

LAW OFFICERS RAID GIANT WHISKEY STILL IN OPERATION

A large moonshine whiskey still was found in the Greene County woods. It was producing more than 800 gallons of moonshine a day. Authorities said the still had probably been running for the past two weeks. It took at least one week to erect the still. Electricity was being used from a nearby house and water was being pumped from a creek several hundred yards away.

WHISKEY, WHISKEY EVERY WHERE AND NOT A DROP TO DRINK

Giant liquor still raided

6. There's a New Sheriff in Town!

THE TITLE OF "HIGH SHERIFF" WAS ORIGINATED IN ENGLAND BY King Alfred to designate the person with jurisdiction over an area. These jurisdictions served as the forerunner of the county system in the United States. The title came to the new world with British settlers but during the early to mid-twentieth century, states began to drop the title. It became more of an official title used infrequently in informal references to a sheriff. Georgia used the title until 1994, being one of the last states to discontinue its use. Even today, Fulton County, Georgia, uses the title unofficially, since it houses the state capital.

After 15 years of chasing down bootleggers and their stills, Wyatt felt he had earned the right to run for sheriff. Some folks thought Wyatt was too young for the office, but it turned out to be an easy win for Wyatt against incumbent Reynolds and candidate Grady Jackson. In January of 1941, L.L. Wyatt was sworn in as the High Sheriff of Greene. And though the police were under the Greene County Commission, no policeman was ever hired that Wyatt didn't approve.

When he was elected, Wyatt moved his family into the apartment at the county jail, which had been built in 1895. Though she was reluctant to leave the home on Walnut Street she had enjoyed, Estelle quickly adjusted to the move. It wasn't long before Wyatt deputized her as jailer so she could deliver prisoners to one of the six cells. She admitted the prisoners to the jail through the door of her kitchen that adjoined the jail.

Estelle cooked outstanding meals for the prisoners—the same meals her family ate. It was rumored that certain folks would try to get locked up just to get a good meal. One could imagine a conversation going something like this: *"This here is some good food—good food,"* one prisoner says. The others agree. *"I declare, sometimes when I'm out there, I get to hankering for Miss Estelle's cookin'. It's almost worth getting thrown in jail for."*

"I grew up in jail," Sonny would say. His friends bragged that they got to spend the night in jail though actually, the bedrooms were *above* the cells. But sleeping in the jail sounded more daring. L.G. "Rooster" Boswell, a friend of Sonny's, said, "I could talk with Wyatt about anything. He made me feel comfortable around him whenever I was in their home." Though Wyatt was a big man, children living in the neighborhood described him as always friendly to them.

Wyatt deputized his son when Sonny was in his teens. From his father, Sonny learned about the relationship between the law and the moonshiner. "For the law, it was like an Indian tracker and his art of looking for the deer tracks. You walked in on a path, 'keeping 'em quiet and keeping 'em low,' looking for signs. You lived off your intelligence network. Everyone was Dad's informant, knocking on his door, dropping off information, or calling on the phone. For you and the moonshiner, it was the fine art of keeping everyone alive. You didn't gain by having someone shot."

Sonny graduated from Greensboro High School and completed his college degree at the University of Georgia. Afterwards, Sonny said, he joined the Army in 1953 "so he could see the world." He served in Germany, India, and Vietnam and earned the rank of Colonel. In 1961, Sonny married Madeleine McDaniel from Cimarron, New Mexico. They had four children who adored Wyatt as much as Sonny did.

His oldest son, Andy, recalled visits with his grandparents: "Granddaddy would squat down to our eye-level, open his arms wide, pockets jingling with change, and ask, 'How are my boys?' Then he would gather all three of us into his arms with an eager embrace."

Wyatt was embraced eagerly, too—by the people of Greene County.

The photo line-up of previous sheriffs of Greene County is short compared to most counties; L.L. Wyatt had a long, successful tenure. One could live in Greene County 36 years and never see a new sheriff.

Wyatt was opposed in only three of the ten elections of his lifetime. He always won. Wyatt asked for the vote, never taking a vote for granted. Everywhere he went, with everybody, Wyatt requested the vote. He already had the respect and the reputation. At election time, Wyatt leveraged his popularity into ballots checked for L.L. Wyatt, Sheriff.

"You never fail to ask for the vote," Wyatt said to Jan Gentry, his administrative assistant. "Asking for the vote" refers to a candidate soliciting a person's promise to vote for him.

"It was just a part of who he was," Jan observed. During a campaign, he might ask the same person two or three times.

"I know you were against me the first time, but I want you to be *for* me next time," Wyatt told one man. It was too late to change the person's mind for the upcoming election, but Wyatt was priming him for the next election four years away!

There were always more voters to convince. "Carey, you play poker with Dewey Newton, don't you? Can you take me out to Dewey's farm?" Wyatt once asked.

"Sure, I'll drive you over there," Carey Williams Jr. answered, wondering why Wyatt wanted to go see somebody who was supporting his opponent for sheriff. When they arrived, Williams was not surprised to find "Bill Duvall for Sheriff" posters all over the place. The signs were planted along the fence facing the road, up the drive, and across the road on a neighbor's property.

Newton was out watering his lawn and spotted the sheriff's car as it arrived. As Wyatt got out of his vehicle, Dewey walked over, speaking first. "Now Sheriff, you know I can't support you this time."

Not to be undone, Wyatt, replied, "That's not why I'm here. I'm here to ask your support in four years."

Despite winning the election, Wyatt was still upset that Bill Duvall had run against him. Duvall's campaign manager was employed at the local Georgia Kraft, Inc. so Wyatt called the head of the company, demanding that he transfer the employee to another county.

"He can stay in Greensboro as long as I want," said the CEO. "We don't mess with your petty politics." The next thing he knew, all the weight trucks for Georgia Kraft were called in and the drivers ticketed. The CEO got the message. He called Wyatt and asked, "Is Rome, Georgia, far enough?"

Four years later, "Wyatt for Sheriff" posters sprang up in the same spots on Dewey Newton's farm.

If the story of Wyatt and Georgia Kraft is true, it seems Wyatt never forgot a political enemy. Though Wyatt did not like to be crossed, he still had an impeccable reputation in the minds of most.

Greene County's 1895 jail with upstairs residence for Sheriff Wyatt's family

Wyatt at 42 years of age

7. The Wyatt Mystique

ANDY WYATT, A GRANDSON OF THE SHERIFF, RAN INTO THE WYATT mystique head-on. Andy came to Greensboro to work at Reynolds Plantation on Lake Oconee for the summer. "The folks at the lake didn't know my family heritage," says Andy, "but as soon as I came into town, I was a celebrity. They even wanted *me* to run for sheriff. It was very hard living up to granddaddy's reputation."

"There's never been a hint of scandal connected with his administration," said one politician who didn't always agree with Wyatt. "He's as honest as the day is long." His honesty set Wyatt apart. He was a man of his word. Folks could count on his doing what he said. Such uncompromising integrity was a huge part of Wyatt's effectiveness. He held the reputation of "honest as the day is long" during his entire tenure in law enforcement.

Wyatt's charisma, too, came from his regard for people. He respected *all* people, rich and poor, black and white, and even criminal. The last thing he ever wanted to do was to hurt someone. He just had a way about him that charmed folks because he approached them with good will. Joel McCray, proprietor of The Greensboro Florists directly across from the courthouse, described Wyatt as "a Southern gentleman, tempered with gentility and respect, even while enforcing the iron-clad law." That Wyatt could balance his allegiance to both garnered respect and awe in return.

Even when arresting someone, Wyatt could be heard saying something like, "Now, you know, I hate to do this to you, but you did break the law. Now, I'll try to do my best by you if you promise not to ever do this again." He did not use handcuffs.

"He seemed to believe that everybody had something good in them," Linda Boswell said as she remembered Wyatt. Linda's father was an attorney in Greensboro during the Wyatt era.

While Wyatt esteemed people above all else, he promoted a strict allegiance to the law at the same time. His ability to do both enabled Wyatt to work magic in enforcing the law. He was a man of the law. Law mattered. Law kept people safe by deterring crime and saving lives. Honor for the law taught children how to function within a community structure. But it was *how* you enforced the law that mattered most to Wyatt.

Wyatt's physical endurance made him seem powerful, too. Andy Wyatt feels he has inherited his grandfather's endurance whenever he runs the Iron Man Competition. "Granddaddy acted as if there was no obstacle he couldn't overcome," said Andy. "He would track the bad guy by car or by foot. You could run, but you could not hide from him."

Wyatt, a 6-foot 1-inch tall policeman who could outrun any bootlegger and a lawman who had survived five or six gun battles, had to have a sturdy body. That physical prowess was sustained even though he often did not stop to eat or sleep. His endurance gave Wyatt the aura of the unstoppable.

Another element of Wyatt's charisma was that he was in control of himself. His demeanor of confidence was part of Wyatt's commanding presence. Coroner Steve McCommons marveled that when Wyatt walked into a situation with his air of confidence, he could immediately bring the emerging crisis under control.

Fearless was the image Wyatt projected; he did not hesitate. Sonny observed, "Dad worked by himself as a policeman and had to live with the results of his actions. There was no one else; he had to be fearless." Wyatt's pervasive presence helped create his mystique. He seemed to be everywhere, anytime. And he almost was. He patrolled the county continuously. He knew everybody in the county. If a new person came into town, Wyatt would make a point to know that person before sunset.

When a new banker moved to Greensboro, a distinguished person walked up to him and said, "Welcome to Greensboro. We're always glad to have good bankers here, especially if they treat my people right." The newcomer had just been greeted by the High Sheriff of Greene.

Wyatt's mystique gave everyone a sense of security. This was especially true of those who seemed to have no one else.

At the hub of life in the Veazey community was Enon Baptist Church, bringing all denominations together for their annual revival meetings, their week of Bible School for children, and their Homecoming with "dinner on the grounds." In the early fifties, the little church began to dwindle as young people left home for more opportunity in the cities.

The church could afford a preacher only twice a month. The other Sundays, the lay members conducted Sunday School and Sunday evening Bible study.

At first, folks liked Edwin Mayford, one of the teachers. Soon, though, Edwin grew long-winded, keeping people later and later–often until 2:00 p.m. He started rambling in his thoughts, too, and folks couldn't follow him well.

The Underwoods, whose large family attended this church, began wondering what was happening to Edwin. They began to leave Sunday School before he stopped his lesson. *Maybe he will get the message.* Some men in the church talked Edwin into giving up the teaching.

One day, Edwin Mayford said to Garner Underwood, "You tell those sons of yours to stop shooting at me with their .22 rifles."

Garner said, "My boys haven't been using a .22 recently."

Edwin insisted, "Yes they have; they been shootin' at me."

Robert Dowds passed by the church on the way to work and noticed Edwin sitting, head in hands, on the steps. Coming back home, Robert found Edwin seated in the same spot. He stopped his car and went to check on Mayford.

"Are you all right, Mr. Mayford?" he asked. Edwin just stared ahead and did not answer. Robert left, worried.

Later, George March passed by the church and recognized Mayford sitting on the steps. He, too, went to talk to him, but Edwin seemed not to hear. George offered to take him home. "You know your wife needs you; she'll be wondering what's happened to you."

"No, I'm not going home," Edwin said.

At this, George rounded up Robert and Johnny Moonson and the three of them returned to approach Edwin. "Mr. Mayford, we are here to help you. You know you need to get back home. One of us will take you if you come with us," George said, reaching out his hand.

"No, I'm not going back there."

"If you won't go home," said March, "we're going to call Sheriff Wyatt. You can't stay out here by yourself." The three waited for a response.

"Well," sighed Edwin, his shoulders sagging, "Whatever *Wyatt* says, I will do." Robert went home to call Wyatt and returned to wait with the others.

Wyatt, ever in command, spoke gently to Edwin, assuring him that he would find a safe place for him if he would come with him. Wyatt helped Edwin down the steps and led him shuffling to the sheriff's car.

Those present waited until Wyatt walked back to ask the men what they thought was going on with Mayford. The men told the sheriff about his recent behavior in church and that Edwin was taking care of an invalid wife while trying to farm.

"Maybe it's just too much for him," George March suggested.

"Well, I think he may have to be taken to Milledgeville to the mental hospital," said Wyatt. "I'll need some of you all to go with me to talk to his family and to sign some papers." The men stated that they would do whatever the sheriff recommended.

At another time, someone called Wyatt to report that Annie Mae was headed down the road with a gun. Wyatt met her on the way. Pulling his car up to her, he rolled down the window and inquired, "Annie Mae, where are you going with that gun?"

Annie Mae, looking determinedly ahead, said, "I'm going to shoot William Lee!" William Lee was her husband with whom she had just had a row.

"You don't want to do that, Annie Mae. Give me the gun," Wyatt said with a firm but gentle voice. She hated to give up the fight, but she guessed Wyatt was right. She handed over the gun. Wyatt then invited her to tell him what was going on.

Such was the individual and the community trust Wyatt's mystique engendered. The Wyatt effect fell over the people he protected like a spell, wrapping them in a blanket of security and trust.

A letter published in the *Atlanta Journal* in 1944 reads:

> ...Believe it or not, here in Georgia there is a county that doesn't have any rackets or crooked politics. It has not always been like this. A few years ago, when you told a bellhop that you wanted a pint of whiskey, he would ask if you wanted "Greene County corn."
>
> Greene County was known for many years for its corn whiskey. The courthouse ring made a mistake and hired a county policeman, and when he took the oath of office, he fulfilled it to the letter. No amount of money could move him, and the famed Greene County bootleggers gave up and moved. This officer is now Sheriff of Greene County.
>
> His honesty caught on, and now all of the county officials down to the city policemen in the different towns of the county are honest men. When you have men in office like the ones in Greene County, there is no need to fear block voting or bought

ballots. If the democracy will work in Greene County, it will work all over the world.

W.F. Barker

There is No Substitute for Experience

8. Who Was This Man?

WYATT'S INNER MAN WAS SUSTAINED IN A WAY FEW UNDERSTOOD. That was the Wyatt few ever questioned. To them, that was just the man he was.

Nancy Webb, Wyatt's office assistant during summers of 1973 and 1974, will never forget. "He had a strong relationship with God behind the facade of self-sufficiency. He tried to treat folks in a Christ-like manner. His inner compass was guided by his relationship with God."

But "Quiet Wyatt," as he came to be known, did not talk about his faith in God; he just lived it. Grandson Andy said, "He had an unshake-able faith in God, which was demonstrated by his life. He believed his mission in life was to take care of the people in Greene County and that God was protecting him to do that. He did not think the bad guys could kill him."

"Whenever Quiet Wyatt did speak, it was worth listening to," Andy added.

Joanne Newsome grew up with Wyatt in and out of her home while her father was Wyatt's deputy. Deputy Archie Newsome passed away of a heart attack at forty-seven years of age, but Wyatt continued to check on her family regularly. Newsome gave this picture of Wyatt: "He had a soft manner and was like a grandfather to us though he was not old enough. He was the most dedicated, humble person I ever knew, but he could be firm, too. He treated others as he wished to be treated. I loved him and Miss Estelle."

Nancy Webb reasoned, "He could not have been in some of the situations he was in if he had not had a strong sense of doing right by people. That came from outside himself, from a higher power. He witnessed his faith in the way he lived his life.

"He left a lasting impression on me, and I feel he did on so many others. I am most grateful. He never reciprocated anger. I would be sitting there, listening to what folks were saying to him and I would think, *Whoa!* But he did not get angry; he maintained respect for the other person."

"Dad never ever raised his voice at me though I deserved it plenty of times," said Sonny, who described himself as a teenage hellion. "After I became an adult, I often envied Dad's quiet, gentle spirit."

"He was not a skirt-chaser," observed Jan Gentry. "You know, like the perception a lot of folks had of police officers of the day."

Greeting Jan on her first day at work, Wyatt said, "Nice to meet you; I'm 71, and you're 17. No one can talk about us!"

"Mr. Wyatt loved Miss Estelle. She was a hemophiliac, so Wyatt was always concerned that Estelle not cut herself when she was preparing food," Jan recalled, "and she liked to cook.

"He had a large, virtually empty office. From his open door, he greeted everyone with a smile and a handshake. And usually, an inquiry into how they and the family were doing. He was like a grandfather."

At the First Baptist Church of Greensboro, Wyatt and Estelle were active members of the Evans Bible Class. It had to be a serious incident for him to leave the worship service.

Rev. Harold Tice, Wyatt's pastor during his later years, was his friend and buddy. Rev. Tice was fascinated with the law, and Wyatt needed a confidante. Wyatt deputized Tice so Tice could accompany the EMTs on their calls.

"Wyatt never ran over anyone," Lewis Duvall said. "He would go to someone and say 'I had a dream that you were… I can't imagine what your momma and daddy would say. If you don't quit, I'll catch you and put you in jail.'"

"Everybody respected him as a good Christian man," Allen Davis commented.

The plaque at the Wyatt Museum reads in part:

> "He was a religious man who believed that God blessed him with protection during all of his fights, gun battles, and dangerous encounters. His law enforcement exploits exposed him to at least five gunshot wounds in the line of duty..."

Wyatt watches to see who is buying large bags of sugar!

9. "These Are My People!"

were his to protect and to keep from running afoul of the law. They were each of value. If he could, he would help them respect the law—for their own good. Perhaps his best work was the number of people he kept *out* of jail by the trust he engendered.

"He had the total confidence of his constituents," Coroner Steve Mc-Commons said, "because he was a man of his word. He would find out the information needed to get a case solved. And he treated even the crook with respect and dignity."

Bobby Voyles, Director Emeritus at Bank South, observed, "The object of Wyatt was not to fill up the jail nor flood the court, but to help folks."

Wyatt banished a notorious mafia man, A.D. Allen, from the county, reprimanding him in front of the press, "These are *my* people, and I want you to leave them alone." Wyatt never, ever resorted to cursing, but this may have been one time he wanted to. A.D. Allen was a well-known thief from Commerce, Georgia. He came to Greensboro one evening and raided a garment factory of its entire inventory. Someone spotted him the next day in town wearing one of the garments!

Sheriff Wyatt located him in Commerce and called A.D.'s brother-in-law to bring A.D. down to Greensboro to post a $60,000 bond for "theft by taking."

The sheriff in Jackson County called Sheriff Wyatt and told him, "A.D. Allen has someone up here that will go his bond, and he won't have to come to Greene County on that, and I will send you the signed bond."

"Go his bond" refers to the purchase of a signed legal document from a third party granting the defendant temporary release and guaranteeing his appearance in court at the set date.

Sheriff Wyatt responded to the Jackson County Sheriff, "I am sorry, but I want A.D. Allen to come to my office, and he will be fingerprinted, and I want to talk to him. Then I will let him go on that signed bond." The next day, A.D. arrived in Greensboro with his brother-in-law.

Before Wyatt brought Allen into the sheriff's office, he called Carey Williams Jr. at *The Herald Journal* to come up to the courthouse. Wyatt took A.D. by his elbow and marched him into his office. There, with Williams as a witness, Wyatt made some things clear to A.D., ending with, "These are *my* people, and I want you to leave them alone!"

A few hours later, Allen's brother-in-law called Wyatt. "Sheriff, what did you do to A.D.? He usually talks his head off, but this afternoon, he said not a word the whole 56 miles back to Commerce."

"Well," said Wyatt, "I made him understand. I put a pistol to his head, and I told him, 'If I ever catch you in Greene County again at night with something that isn't yours, I will kill you.' And I had the newspaper editor here to witness the conversation."

Allen did as he was told and was never seen in Greene again. A.D. Allen, Daniel Warren, and Wayman Patrick were convicted of a kidnapping and robbery near Griffin, Georgia, in December of 1973. They were sentenced to life in prison. Allen received a prison term of 87 years.

"Two fellows hated the ground Wyatt walked on," prominent Greene County dairyman Lewis Duvall said, "He put them out of business. One of them was the liquor king of the county. The other one went to prison. Wyatt ruled the county." The "other one" was A.D., who called Wyatt "the meanest man that ever lived."

Wyatt took care of people by protecting their reputations. Prince Parrish, as Fire Chief of Greene, was often called to a scene to assist Wyatt. Once, Prince received a late night call.

"Prince," said Wyatt, "looks like we have a friend out here on the river asleep in his car. Can you get someone to come out with you and drive him home?" The friend was a well-known citizen whom Wyatt was saving from embarrassment.

A black man who had been jailed was scheduled to sing at a big church meeting in town. The rest of the quartet had been searching the county for the fourth member of their group. When they located him in jail, they pled their case.

"Mister Sheriff, is there any way you can let LeRoy out to sing with us just for tonight? This is the biggest booking we ever had. Please, Sheriff?"

Wyatt said, "Sure, I'll let him out for that. But first, he's got to show me he can sing tenor."

The incarcerated man, together with the other three members of the quartet, raised the rafters of the jail with *Swing Low, Sweet Chariot*, *When the Roll is Called up Yonder* and *Amazing Grace*. The men in the other cells broke into a round of applause.

Wyatt said, "Have LeRoy back in three hours or I'll be looking for all four of you." Wyatt was about extending good will to his people.

Often, if someone was incarcerated and could not pay the fines, Wyatt would go to a businessman and ask if "Mr. Randall Smith" could work off his fine with them. Sometimes the jailed person found a regular job waiting for him when he was released.

"I'm having to arrest you, Eddie," Wyatt said in an apologetic tone to Eddie Sarden Jr. one day. Eddie admitted to having had an altercation with someone in Athens.

Sarden, a black man, continued his story, "Wyatt was a nice guy; he treated me like I was a human being. He explained everything to me. Sheriff said he would take me to Athens for the hearing; he would get someone to go my bond; and he would get someone to give me a job so I could pay off my fine. I spent one night in jail, and then I was out, and Wyatt did everything just like he said he would."

"Sheriff Wyatt," Eddie added, "was a good man. He didn't come after me with guns and kicking the door down. He treated me like I was somebody."

Sometimes Wyatt's task was extremely urgent.

Miss Steeling had left a note on the drug store counter. The druggist picked up the piece of paper and read, "I'm going out to commit suicide." The druggist had noticed that she seemed distressed and wondered why she was buying ether. He immediately called Wyatt with a description. Wyatt called Prince Parrish to assist him. Prince took a volunteer with him, knowing that Miss Steeling would be upset when they tried to stop her. They drove out in the direction they thought she had headed.

When they met the mailman en route, Prince asked if he had seen a green 1953 Chevrolet. "Yes," said Charles O'Kelley, "that car passed me just about twenty minutes ago, headed in that direction." Charles pointed east across the field, and Prince and his volunteer speeded up.

Soon they found the Chevrolet. They opened the door, took the bottle of ether out of Steeling's hand, and started her car. Sure enough, as Steeling woke up, she began crying and screaming, "Leave me alone; let me go." The volunteer restrained her while Prince drove them to meet Wyatt. The sheriff transported her to the hospital in Athens, giving her a listening ear as he drove. Miss Steeling recovered, began to live a full life, got married, and was a productive citizen.

Wyatt was called to the scene of an accident behind Goldstein's Store on Main Street. A worker, Henry Carver, was lifting some heavy equipment when it slipped and severed an artery in the man's neck. Wyatt placed his own finger over the injury to stop the flow of blood and walked Henry two and a half blocks to the doctor, holding his finger on Henry's neck all the way. There was no such thing as EMTs at that time in Greensboro. Wyatt didn't do too well at tipping his hat to the ladies on that trip.

Perhaps nothing illustrates Wyatt's sense of justice more than this hand-typed letter:

May 23, 1961

State Board of Pardons and Paroles
State Capitol
Atlanta, Georgia

Dear Lady and Gentlemen:

This letter comes in behalf of Mr. Jim E. Jones who is now serving a sentence from the Superior Court of Fulton County for defrauding the State of Georgia during the Administration of Governor Griffin.

I have known Mr. Jones for some fifteen years. During said time I was closely associated with him by virtue of me being Sheriff of Greene County, and he being with the Georgia Bureau of Investigation. We have worked on many cases together on a great number of ocassions. I have been in his home and he in mine.

I always found Mr. Jones to be an honest, efficient and reliable law enforcement officer and a man of sterling character.

All I know about his trial and the ultimate sentence imposed upon him is what I have read in the papers. It has always been hard for me to believe that he was guilty of the things of which he was charged. However, during my experience of more than thirty-five years as a law enforcement officer, I have seen good men get involved in situations entirely repugnant to their nature through the influence of associates.

I believe in the administration of justice to all persons and all classes equally. There has been numerous charges of similar nature against other persons connected with the Griffin Administration, but I know of no other individual who has been accused of crime against the State during said Administration who is serving time.

I think it is within the provence of your Board to correct and adjust unreasonable sentences and to, as nearly as possible, see that all persons of a particular class are treated equally for the same or similar offences. Mr. Jones is bearing the burden for all who have been similar accused.

I will certainly appreciate any consideration you can give to Mr. Jones at this time; and I am sure beyond a doubt such consideration will be well justified as Mr. Jones can and will be a credit to his family and to society if given the opportunity.

With kindest regards, I am

Sincerely,

L.L. Wyatt

Letter to Parole Board, typed and signed by Wyatt

10. The High Sheriff Rides Alone

THE SHERIFF WAS BY LAW IN CHARGE OF THE COURTHOUSE, COL-
lecting taxes, holding elections, ensuring school bus safety, handling
traffic violations, enforcing the law, and presiding over the court. He
was commander of the militia in most counties. In the South, the High
Sheriff was traditionally viewed as one of the county's most influential
political office holders. In the County Greene, he had to do it by himself.
He had little help at first. Today, the sheriff is still seen as the Chief Law
Enforcement Officer in all 159 counties in Georgia.

To some who worked closest with him, Wyatt could be intimidating.
He knew everything that happened in the courthouse and pretty much
the entire county. He was aware of what occurred in the ordinary's office.
Traffic citations stayed with the sheriff. The fines were paid to his office;
he would locate folks, so they had to pay up. Today the fines go to the
court. He was a good friend of Ed Brown, judge of the Ordinary Court,
later named the Probate Court, who was in charge of civil law. Brown
would represent clients charged by Wyatt. They thought alike.

Judge Brown said of Wyatt, "He has always gone beyond the call of
duty and been a detective, policeman, prohibition officer, traffic cop, or
whatever else he could do to help out. He's always done about four jobs;
Greene County got a bargain in him."

Laverne Ogletree was Clerk of Court to Judge Brown. "You could
set your clock by Wyatt's precise schedule," Ogletree said. "Wyatt parked
on Court Street. He arrived at the courthouse each morning at 8:00 a.m.
and raised the flag. At 10:00 a.m., he walked to the post office. At 12:00

noon, the sheriff left the office to have lunch at home with Estelle. He was back at 1:00 p.m. and at 5:00 p.m., he returned to lower the flag."

The courthouse building was never locked, even at night, and windows were always open during the day. The courthouse was small with close quarters during Wyatt's time. In 1997, an addition, compatible with the original, was added and the old courthouse was rehabilitated and restored, according to historical standards, to its former appearance. Greene County's courthouse is the third oldest in Georgia and is on the National Historic Register.

"There were things in law enforcement that Wyatt didn't like. He wanted the system to be respected, so he had his way of cleaning things up. He wanted to create a better image of law enforcement," said Probate Judge Ogletree, who was probably the youngest person to be elected to a Constitutional Office (an office fixed by the state constitution) in Greene County. Laverne added, "I always felt that Sheriff Wyatt thought I was too young for the job of Clerk of Probate and that the job should be held by a man." Ogletree was elected Probate Judge when Judge Roper, who followed Brown, resigned. Her office was near Wyatt's so she could hear everything, even if she didn't want to.

When Laverne Ogletree was Clerk of the Ordinary Court, she spotted a beautiful pine table in a side room of the court that was infrequently used. Laverne began to covet that table for her office, where she worked on a hard metal table. She thought it through and took the risk.

While Wyatt was out of the office for lunch, Laverne rushed outside to the bench in front of the courthouse. "I need three of y'all to help me move some tables around in the courthouse," Laverne said.

"All right, we'll help you," said one of the men as he motioned to two friends. "Let's go help the lady."

Once inside, Laverne explained, "What I need is for you to take this heavy metal table up those two flights of stairs and exchange it for a wooden one. I'll show you."

She was hurrying the men as they kept asking, "Does the sheriff know about this?" She told them not to worry, but they worried anyway. "I don't know about this if the sheriff don't know we're doing this," one of the men said.

"It'll be okay," Laverne kept reassuring them. They huffed and puffed as they lugged that metal table up the steps, at the same time looking over their shoulders for any sign of Wyatt.

It was an easier task bringing the wooden table down. As soon as they set the table in Ogletree's office, the men tumbled over each other in their haste to leave, scared to death that Wyatt would appear, and they'd be in trouble. Laverne managed to get a few coins to each of them before they disappeared.

When Wyatt returned, Laverne was fast at work. Wyatt stood there, shifting change from one hand to the other, as was his habit when he was thinking. He looked first at the table and then at Laverne. But he never said a word. Neither did she. That table is still in use in the Archives office of the courthouse today.

And Laverne continued to serve as Judge of Probate Court. Judge Ogletree smiled as she remembered the "uniform" that identified Wyatt: "A sheriff always in his white shirt, black suit and tie, and black wide-brimmed hat. Short-sleeved shirt in summer." He stayed ready for the line of duty. "The Man in Black" is how some referred to Wyatt.

One of the many responsibilities assigned the Man in Black was overseeing the safety of the school buses. "Hey, Rooster," said Wyatt to Sonny's friend one day, "I need a school bus driver out there on your route. So many men have been drafted for the war, I don't have a driver for the school bus out your way. You've been driving all that equipment there on your daddy's farm, why don't you drive that route?" World War II was coming to an end, but the men were not yet home.

Rooster was fourteen years old! But the High Sheriff had called. Rooster drove the route for two years. Wyatt trusted L.G. "Rooster" Boswell to be responsible. The sheriff was in charge of annual inspections of all the buses before the school year began. "Now, Rooster, you just bring that bus in here, and I'll take care of the inspection for you," Wyatt assured him.

Wyatt's office was just inside the front door of the courthouse. He sat in a swivel chair, behind a long table, engaging all who stuck their heads through the doorway.

"How are your cows doing? Tell me how many you have now," Wyatt would ask, making a point to inquire about each person's welfare as they stopped to greet him.

"Every morning, folks gathered at the courthouse and circulated around Wyatt's office to learn the news of the County," Prince Parrish, former Fire Chief, said. "One day, a black couple came up. Wyatt excused himself from the bunch and went out to see what the couple wanted. Wyatt treated them the same as he would have had they been white."

Nancy Webb, former secretary in Wyatt's office, described him as, "a kind gentleman with quite a wonderful way with people. He always seemed to have the right words, the right demeanor. He was soft spoken, but he could be stern at the same time. And he had a good sense of humor.

"Even when you had done something wrong, he still had a caring attitude toward you. He cared about his family, went home for lunch each day. He looked forward to Sonny's and Madeleine's coming to visit. He would take his grandchildren to the bank to show them the vault."

After lunch at home one day, Nancy came back to work with red, puffy eyes. She had tried to pull herself together by splashing water on her face, but when she entered the office, Wyatt noticed. She had to tell him.

"I just got a letter from the Medical College of Georgia's School of Nursing in Augusta informing me that I was not accepted for the scholarship," Nancy sobbed. "I don't have any other way to go to college."

Nancy dropped her head into her hands, trying to stop the crying. She wiped her eyes with her hands and then grabbed a tissue and blew her nose, clearly embarrassed.

"Well, now, Nancy, you run home and get that letter and let me take a look."

Nancy could hardly believe that Wyatt wanted to help. She began to get control of herself as she sped her car over the four miles to her house, grabbed the letter, and swiftly made her way back to the office. Nancy handed Wyatt the letter.

"Go down to Hunter's Drug Store and get us two cokes," Wyatt said as he took two quarters out of the drawer and handed them to Nancy. Ten minutes later, Nancy walked back into the office with the cokes. She heard Wyatt on the phone saying, "I know this young lady; she's a fine person. She needs financial assistance to attend. This is her first year of nursing school."

Two weeks afterward, Nancy got a second letter. This time, it was a notification that she would receive a full scholarship and financial aid package. Nancy was able to attend the first class of the Medical College's School of Nursing on the University of Georgia campus.

"Without Wyatt's help, I would not have gone to college," Nancy Webb said with gratitude.

"Just dropping by to say hi," Nancy would say to Wyatt whenever she was home from college. She usually found him sitting at his old roll-top desk, plucking on the manual typewriter with his index finger. "He would grin when he realized I had caught him trying to type," Nancy said. That roll-top desk, restored to its original beauty, now sits in the Sonny Wyatt home, treasured for its memories.

Jan Gentry, too, noted how Wyatt engaged folks as they passed his office. One day a mother with several rowdy children passed by. The mother was trying to corral a boy of seven. She yelled at him, "Billy Bob, you better behave yo'self. If you don't do what I tell you, that High Sheriff in there's gonna' get you." As she pointed to the sheriff's office, Wyatt arose from his chair and walked out into the hall.

"Now, Irene, don't tell your child that," Wyatt advised the mother gently. "We are your children's friends. If they get into trouble, who are they going to turn to if they are afraid of the deputy and me?" Irene threw her hand over her mouth and, grabbing Billy Bob's arm, snuck guiltily away. She had been caught in the act by the High Sheriff himself!

Back in the office, Wyatt sat down and shook his head, saying to Jan, "Why do parents do that? There are two things parents should teach their children. One is that the sheriff and his deputies are their children's friends. The other is that all guns are loaded guns. There is no such thing as an unloaded gun when a child is present."

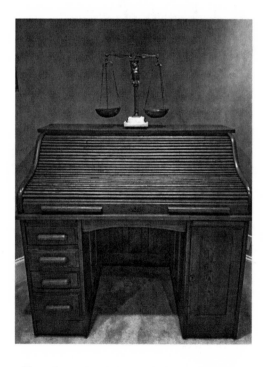

The roll-top desk Wyatt used in the courthouse

Sheriff Wyatt sworn-in again as Sheriff of Greene County in 1973 by Judge Edward P. Brown.

Judge Brown swears in Wyatt in 1973

11. Sometimes You Have to "Blow 'Em Out!"

WYATT LOVED HIS CARS, SO MUCH SO THAT FOLKS WERE WILLING to wait to buy a Wyatt-pre-owned car.

Jan Gentry recalled, "The only time he ever got aggravated at Estelle was when she was driving."

"Estelle never drives over 40 miles an hour," Jan remembered Wyatt saying. "She never blows it out. You do need to blow 'em out every now and then."

"Blow 'em out" refers to a recommended practice during the fifties of clearing out the motor by running wide open.

One of Wyatt's favorite activities was taking family guests out on his patrol circuits. His grandchildren loved getting to go out with their sheriff granddaddy. Madeleine, their mom, recalled a ride one day with some out-of-town guests. This time, Estelle got aggravated at Wyatt's driving.

Estelle exclaimed, "Wyatt, you're driving so fast, they're not seeing *anything!*"

As they rode along on the unpaved roads, Madeleine and the grandchildren would listen to him talk over his radio and to those he met along the way.

"Sometimes when I was in the car with Wyatt and he would stop to greet someone on the back roads," said Madeleine, "he talked in a dialect my New Mexico ear could not decipher."

"He spoke in a jargon that was totally unintelligible to me," said grandson Andy.

"Sometimes, Granddaddy would stop out on Highway 44 at a country church whose pastor was his friend. Granddaddy would let us go behind the church to the back side of their parking lot and shoot 22s at tin cans," Andy added.

Wyatt never drove a police car, always an unmarked car. "When I worked for him, he had a blue LTD," said Jan Gentry. "And he advised my daddy to get me a car I didn't want. I had picked out a white Monte-Carlo with red trim. Wyatt talked my dad into getting me a used buttered-rum Ford! Being practical, I kept it for years, but I didn't like that buttered-rum color."

"Wyatt bought his own cars. He always drove dark blue or black Fords, unmarked. Just as he preferred a tiny badge, Wyatt preferred to keep his siren inside the car. And I always found that gun under the driver's seat. You know he wanted to have to walk back to the car for it if he needed it," said Allen Davis, who serviced Wyatt's cars at the Ford Motor Company in Greensboro.

Richard Moon, manager of the Ford Motor Company, often worked the evening shift. One Friday night, Wyatt and Newsome whipped into the Ford place, all steamed up. They had been chasing a two-seater coupe loaded with whiskey when the temperature needle on Wyatt's car shot up to "Hot" underlined in red. Wyatt stopped the car and checked under the hood. The boiling water was evaporating fast. Wyatt didn't have a spare jug of water in the car, but he did have plenty jugs of moonshine, confiscated earlier. Wyatt unscrewed a jug and filled the radiator with the 'shine.'

They made it back to town at 173 degrees Fahrenheit! Richard had to wait a few minutes for the steam to die down. When he finally got the hot cap off, Richard was engulfed in a geyser of boiling alcohol fumes.

"I was standing there trying to get water poured into that tank and getting drunker by the minute. I inhaled so many moonshine fumes, I was as 'high as a Georgia pine,'" Richard said.

One evening, Wyatt got to drive a Cadillac, and he drove it about as fast as if he were on duty. Only he was driving that Cadillac up to the foothills of the Sangre de Cristo Mountains of New Mexico.

"I remember that trip well," Madeleine said. "I had driven down from Cimarron to the Albuquerque Airport to pick up Sonny's parents who were arriving in New Mexico for our wedding in 1961. Wyatt asked if he could drive the shiny 1958 Cadillac Sedan DeVille. He was like a child with a coveted toy. He put his foot on the accelerator and we were flying low!

"I was holding my breath, hoping we wouldn't get stopped for speeding. Then I realized a sheriff was driving, so I would probably be all right. Suddenly the lights went out. It is dark out there on the New Mexico highways when the lights go out. Wyatt's foot came right off the accelerator for a moment, and then the lights came back on. We were soon flying low again for the rest of the 215 miles. Even when we got into the foothills around Cimarron, he was above the speed limit. Wyatt loved every minute of the drive. Luckily, for most of the trip, the roads are relatively straight, and there was not much traffic." Wyatt now knew why the Cadillac motor was the engine of choice for moonshine haulers in revving up their autos.

Wyatt could be seen flying low in his Fords, too. One lady needed a ride to Thomson, Georgia, to renew her driver's license. Wyatt offered to drive her over. When asked how her trip with the sheriff went, the lady replied, "I never knew before today that you could *fly* from Greensboro to Thomson!"

Allen Davis bought one of Wyatt's Fords. It came with an unusual accessory: a brick in the back window where someone had thrown it when Wyatt was breaking up a fight.

Ellis Morgan worked at the Greensboro Ford Motor Company with

Grover Torbert. One day, Wyatt dropped his car off for a check-up and walked the block to the courthouse. Mid-morning, Wyatt picked up his car. At 1:30 in the afternoon, here comes Wyatt again with his vehicle. It was a 1956 Ford with a 110-gauge speedometer and a 312 V-8 engine.

Wyatt got out and said, "You boys didn't get it quite right. I was going up that Geissler Hill over there, and the car just doesn't have the 'oomph' I need. I'm gonna leave it here and let you check it out again. See if you can give it some more power." As soon as Wyatt was out of the shop, Grover said to Ellis, "Just park it over there in the back corner. I'm not even going to raise the hood. There's nothing wrong with that car." It sat in the same spot until Wyatt returned just before closing time.

"Okay, Mr. Wyatt, let me get your car for you," Grover said, turning to go before any questions could be asked. He brought the car to the front of the shop and said, "Sheriff, here are your keys. I hope it's all right now."

Next day, Wyatt dropped by again, rolled his window down, and with all smiles, said, "Well, boys, I think you got it that time. It's just right! Thank you."

The "boys" were all smiles, too, as Wyatt drove off.

Wyatt needed well-serviced cars for the high-speed chases he sometimes found himself in. He survived two such chases, which totaled two of his Fords. One of the chases left him unconscious in the back seat of what was left of his auto. That's where he landed after the car hit an embankment, hidden in a cloud of dust intentionally stirred up by the fleeing bootlegger, flipped over and landed on all fours. He did not know what had happened until the next morning. Speed was part of his job. And God watched out for Wyatt in the dust of the chases, just as He watched out for him at the end of a gun.

Wyatt on Patrol

Sonny and Madeleine's wedding photo with Sheriff and Mrs. Wyatt
and Mr. and Ms. McDaniel, Madeleine's parents

12. Strange Things Happen in The Land of Greene

THE HEADLINE IN THE *Augusta Chronicle*, FEB. 17, 1958, READ, "Safe Stolen! Owner Says It's Empty!" It seemed that thieves stole a 250-pound safe from Whit's place. The two thieves had pried their way into the store with a crowbar. They took a gun from the store and lugged a safe out into the sub-zero weather. Sheriff Wyatt and H. Whitley, the owner, had a big laugh when Whitley told Wyatt, "There was not a penny in that safe!"

* * *

Tom Moore ran a general store in White Plains. Every week, he sent eggs to a lady in Greensboro. Once, as Wyatt was leaving the store, he asked, "Sheriff, would you do me a favor and drop these eggs off at Ms. Topping's for me?"

"Sure thing," said the sheriff. Along with the eggs went two pints of contraband whiskey. Folks still believe that the sheriff who knew everything never knew.

Likewise, a Sunday School teacher, dubbed the "Buttermilk Lady", sold moonshine in the middle of downtown Greensboro on Saturdays when the streets were full of shoppers. She was resourceful. She painted her pint jars white, put them into a milk basket and sold her "buttermilk" on the streets. Her milk had a reputation with some folks as the best in the state.

Someone asked her, "Josie, what you gonna' do if Wyatt comes along and wants to buy your 'milk'?"

Josie answered, "I keep two pints of the real stuff in my basket, just in case!"

* * *

Wyatt had just bought himself a brand new car. His deputy drove it out to a home where a wild party was going on. Wyatt hid in the back seat of the car. The deputy went to the door with a warning. "Sheriff says y'all need to break up your partyin' and your drinkin' that moonshine. You're disturbin' the peace."

The drinking did not stop. Wyatt returned an hour later. He heard shouting and cursing and loud noises, indications the party was getting wilder. Wyatt knocked on the door. When the host made it to the door, Wyatt padlocked the house with the host and his guests inside. The sheriff gave them an ultimatum. "I want you to drink *all* the moonshine in the house. When you've finished it off, I'll come back and release you." He posted a deputy to secure the place.

Next day when Wyatt went to free them, the host said to the sheriff, "I promise I'll never do that again. They nearly killed each other. And look how they trashed my place!"

* * *

Out in the Daniel Springs area, speedy-on-his-feet Wyatt was chasing a bootlegger. Up and down the hilly terrain of the woods they went for two or three miles. They crossed a stream; the bootlegger made it up to the top of the hill beyond and flopped down to rest. He hollered to Wyatt, "Hey, Sheriff, let's take a rest."

Wyatt, about a fourth of a mile behind, sloshed through the stream below and stopped to rest also. After a few minutes, the bootlegger yelled down to Wyatt again, "Hey, Sheriff, I'm ready when you is!"

* * *

Bill Callaway of Atlanta had driven to Greensboro to visit relatives. Bill reported to Wyatt that his rifles and guns were missing from his car after he attended a baseball game in Greensboro. Wyatt said he would be on the lookout for them.

The next day, Wyatt called Bill. "Got your guns," Wyatt said.

"How'd you find them so fast?" Bill asked.

"I was walking to church, and I spotted a boy walking down the other side of the street. When he saw me, he dropped his head to avoid eye contact. I went over and stopped him. When I questioned him, he confessed and took me out to see where he had buried the guns."

Another time, Wyatt was at Henry Airs's store. Henry sold all kinds of illegal stuff from time to time. Outside the store, with his foot on a whiskey barrel holding three guns, the sheriff said, "You know, I know you're selling guns out here; if you don't stop, Henry, I'm gonna get you."

* * *

Nellie Lee McLeod once called Wyatt. The sheriff happened to be in Atlanta, but he returned the call, "Nellie, how you doing? You got a problem out there?"

Nellie told him she thought someone was trying to get into her house. It sounded as if they were fiddling with the doorknob. She was afraid to leave her house to go to work.

"I'm standing here with my gun looking out the window for him," Nellie said, "and I'm not afraid to shoot him if I see him coming toward my house."

"Nellie, don't you know you can't shoot someone *out there*? They have to be entering your home first."

"Sheriff, are you crazy or something?" Nellie asked incredulously. "I'll have him *inside* by the time you can get here!"

Every time Wyatt saw Nellie after that, he would ask, "Nellie, you been dragging any bodies over your threshold lately?"

* * *

One of the strangest bodies that ever came to Greensboro would become a curious and sad legend.

Someone found a man severely injured along the railroad tracks on the Madison Highway just outside of Greensboro. It was 1937. There was no hospital, so he was taken to the jail where he could be seen after. The county nurse came to the cell regularly to take care of the man.

The nurse eventually took him into her home to better care for him. After a week or two, he passed away. McCommons Funeral Home took him into their possession, embalmed him, dressed him in a suit and named him "Oscar." McCommons advertised in papers all over, and fingerprints were sent to the FBI. People did come to see if he were their long-lost loved one, but there were never any matches.

Oscar "lived" in a casket in the McCommons Funeral Home for 25 years. A glass top was placed over the coffin so Oscar could be seen more easily. High school students would skip out at lunch and go see Oscar, weaving tales about his long nails and hair to frighten their classmates. It was a rite of passage for seniors to visit Oscar before graduating from high school. At Halloween, McCommons stayed open so kids could come by to see Oscar.

McCommons kept hoping to locate Oscar's family for him. An official from the Department of Health came by with some questions.

"Is it true that you have a man here who died 15 years ago?" asked the inspector of McCommons.

"No, sir," answered McCommons, "he died *25* years ago!" The inspector ordered McCommons to give Oscar a proper burial.

Greene County's legend of Oscar is rivaled only by that of L.L. Wyatt. Oscar, however, was a better night watchman for McCommons Funeral Home than Wyatt could ever have been!

Deputy Reese Smith, editor Carey Williams, Jr.,
and Union Point police chief Carlton Lewis honor Wyatt

13. Politicking 365 Days a Year

WYATT DID NOT LIKE POLITICIANS, YET HE POLITICKED CEASE-lessly. Known as "the consummate politician", he was at it around the clock. The sheriff and Estelle made appearances at most annual church homecoming dinners, and at most funerals, black and white. At times, he would have his deputy drive him by the church slowly for all to see. Or perhaps to see if things were peaceful. The folks of Greene looked forward to getting a handshake from the High Sheriff when he came around.

So influential was Wyatt that his support was sought by persons such as Sam Nunn, Carl Sanders, Lester Maddox, and Bo Callaway as they announced for office.

"Mr. Wyatt just was always about making folks like him," said Jan Gentry.

Wyatt was the first to qualify for each sheriff's election. Several days ahead of the date qualifications were due, he would have his paperwork ready to file. And he would be the first in line for his new tag.

Folks just breaking into politics or those seeking to move up enlisted the backing of L.L. Wyatt. Wyatt was in the middle of the state and was key to directing the candidates to the folks they needed to see in the surrounding counties.

Carl Sanders sought Wyatt's political weight as he campaigned in 1961 to become Georgia's next governor. Becoming governor in 1962, Sanders paid tribute to Wyatt "for your loyal, dedicated, and effective work throughout the campaign." Sanders appointed Wyatt a member of the State Department of Public Safety in 1963.

Wyatt received an invitation to go behind the Iron Curtain in 1964 as a member of the Georgia Law Enforcement Officials Delegation to tour England, Belgium, Poland, Hungary, Germany, and The Soviet Union. The self-financed trip was to compare law enforcement methods and procedures in those countries with those in Georgia. There is no indication that Wyatt participated in this opportunity.

In 1965, Howard "Bo" Callaway, Republican candidate for governor of Georgia, was in Greensboro on his way to the Augusta Nationals. He spent the night at the home of Carey Williams Sr. The next day, Wyatt knocked on the door of their home. Carey Jr. answered.

"Hey, Carey, I heard Bo Callaway was at your house. I want to see him," Wyatt requested. Carey went inside, brought Callaway out, and introduced Wyatt to him. They spoke a few minutes, and then Wyatt pulled out a handful of large bills and handed them to Callaway.

In 1965, too, Democrat gubernatorial candidate, Lester Maddox, staged a backward-bicycling event in Greensboro between himself and Rayfield Williams, a black citizen of Greene, known for his skill in riding. The event drew 2500 people and the grandstanding brought Maddox the political attention he needed. Though Rayfield lost, Maddox awarded him the now famous bicycle.

As the crowd thinned out, and there were no more hands to shake, Maddox spoke to Carey Williams Jr. "Hey, Carey," Maddox said, "can you take me up to see Wyatt? I want to ask him to donate to my campaign."

"Well," answered Carey, "I don't know about that. Wyatt is a pretty scrupulous person. I don't know if you can get anything from him."

"Let's go see," said Maddox. Carey Jr. walked Maddox up Main Street to the courthouse and introduced him to Wyatt. Carey retreated to a bench in the hallway. Thirty minutes later, a grinning Maddox emerged with cash in hand. As he left, Wyatt reminded Maddox, "Now, I want to be Peace Officer of the Year–remember?"

In 1972, Sam Nunn, already a member of Georgia's House of Representatives, decided to run for U. S. Senate from Georgia. He headed to Greene County to see Sheriff Wyatt. Nunn was one of a very few politicians Wyatt publicly endorsed. Four years later, Wyatt hung a photograph of himself with Sam Nunn taken when now Senator Nunn spent Memorial Day, 1976, in Greensboro. Nunn was the only politician whose photo ever hung on the walls of Wyatt's office.

Wyatt made a prophetic prediction to the Senator. "I feel you will go down in history as one of Georgia's greatest politicians." Nunn retired in 1996 with national honor and recognition just as Wyatt had predicted.

Wyatt also politicked for local folks. He would handpick people and recommend them. He might tell the Commission, "I think Stone would make a good Commissioner." Or he might say, "How about Boswell as a Bank Director? Or Foster for School Superintendent? Or Voyles for Chair of Deacons at the church? Or Duvall for President of Lion's Club?"

Ray Marchman became Clerk of Court in 1977. Ray had established a habit of attending the funerals of the customers and vendors of his store. Wyatt, who showed up at funerals too, said, "Ray, you keep going to those funerals and smiling at folks, you can be Clerk of Court as long as you want." Ray was a nephew of Willard Taylor.

Wyatt's voice was respected in political and business circles as well as in law enforcement. He was a member of First Baptist Church in Greensboro, a member of the Lions Club, a member of the San Marino Masonic Lodge in Greensboro, and served as a Director of the Citizens Union Bank in Greensboro. He was vice-president of the 10th District Peace Officers Association and a member of the Georgia Law Officers Association and the Sheriff's Association.

In these circles, Wyatt might say, "I don't think that'd be a wise thing to do." In a quiet, friendly way, he would exhibit his strong will.

Wyatt served informally as the local Credit Bureau since the nearest bureau was in Athens. Wyatt knew everyone in the county, so creditors came to him for references.

Carey Williams Jr. summed it up: "Wyatt was the best politician I ever knew. He practiced politics daily and was a master at it."

Sheriff L. L. Wyatt welcomes United States Senator Sam Nunn to Greensboro on Memorial Day in May 1976. Senator Nunn had strong support in Greene County from Sheriff Wyatt. The only picture that hung in the Sheriff's Office was a picture of Senator Sam Nunn and Sheriff Wyatt. Sheriff Wyatt called Sam Nunn the next politican in Georgia to fill the late Richard B. Russell's shoes, in honor and respect.

The Sheriff and the Senator

73

Re-Elect

L. L. WYATT

SHERIFF

Greene County

CARL E. SANDERS
405 STATE CAPITOL
ATLANTA 3, GEORGIA

Dear Mr. Wyatt:

I've thought of you on many occasions since election
night, but the press of official duties has been so
great that I am just now finding time to handle my
personal correspondence. I have found that a Governor-
Nominate has very little time of his own. Each day
seems to bring a new crop of crises.

I do want you to know that I shall be forever grateful
for your loyal, dedicated and effective work throughout
the campaign. Our hard-earned victory is indeed a
tribute to you and your fellow workers who gave so
unselfishly of their time and energy.

Now that things have settled down a bit, I hope to
have time to visit with my many friends throughout
the State. In the meantime, whenever you are in
Atlanta, please consider this your personal invitation
to come by and visit with us at our office here in
the State Capitol.

Betty asks that I express her heartfelt thanks to you
and joins me in sending our kindest personal regards.

Cordially,

Honorable L. L. Wyatt
Sheriff, Green County
Greensboro, Georgia

November 6, 1962

Letter of Thanks from Governor Sanders

75

14. Each Life Matters

WYATT LIVED BY THE CODE THAT EACH LIFE MATTERED. L.L. WY-att, long before integration, saw blacks as people who counted. The black community both trusted him and feared him. But they could sleep at night if they were not breaking the law.

Many black people lived in a section of Greensboro called Canaan where their families settled after emancipation. Canaan, located on the Veazey-Greensboro road, was on the edge of town. Most residences were small houses or two-story apartments. Often, one could see people milling around the apartments or sitting in straight back chairs under the shade trees, especially on weekends when everybody was home from work and had time to visit friends.

Once, an argument broke out in Canaan between two young men. The argument escalated into a fight as more men got involved. It was getting heated and becoming scarier. A passerby called Wyatt.

Wyatt walked into the crowd. The men all backed away, and the fight was over. The sheriff had not said a word. He just looked at the ones swinging at each other. They recognized that look. They had better stop while they had a chance, or they'd be "under the jail."

The black community feared Wyatt, but they relied on his fairness. He had proved to be their friend. He went to their churches and to their funerals. As he got to know them, people found they could talk to Wyatt, and he would listen to get the whole story. The black people trusted Wyatt more than they did almost anyone else because he looked out for them.

Wyatt grew up poor himself so he understood poverty. He had lived on a farm where he sometimes worked with black folks side by side. They were his people, too.

But he didn't spare the law. Wyatt spotted a car weaving in and out of the U.S. 278/Broad Street traffic. He pulled the car over. Wyatt walked up to the car and motioned the driver to roll down the window. Sitting behind the wheel was a prominent civil rights leader, driving home from a march in Sandersville, Georgia, a few counties away. Wyatt could smell the alcohol on his breath. Wyatt introduced himself as the sheriff of Greene County and asked for his driver's license.

"Mr. Civil Rights Leader," said Wyatt, "it's obvious from your traffic pattern and the smell of alcohol on your person that you have been driving drunk. Am I right?"

The driver could not hide. He admitted to being under the influence while at the wheel and said, "I just want to get home." He might have attempted to have the ticket torn up had he known he was being stopped for drunk driving in the former moonshine capital of the state.

"Tell you what, Mr. Civil Rights Leader, I could give you a ticket and arrest you, but I'd rather make a deal. If you promise *never, ever* to bring a civil rights march to Greene County, I'll let you go." Mr. C.R. Leader agreed to the deal. Wyatt took the offender over to the jail where he called the man's family to come down to Greensboro and drive him home. Wyatt waited with the leader, perhaps charming him with tales of his moonshine cleanup days and maybe slipping in a story or two of what happens to people driving drunk.

Whether the pact was a good deal for the black people of Greene is debatable. But Wyatt was about keeping the peace and protecting the people. No one would be arrested in Greene County for civil disobedience. There would be no torching or burning buildings in Greene County if the march got out of hand. Wyatt may have reasoned, too, that often black people get hurt in the process. They would be the ones going

77

to prison, paying fines, and losing badly needed jobs if businesses were trashed.

A black woman, Mrs. Emma Davis, was once photographed and interviewed for a newspaper article on Wyatt. Holding up one of Wyatt's campaign posters, she said, "The first man I ever voted for was Wyatt in 1940." She voted for him every sheriff's election. Voting when she was 103 years old, she said, "Sheriff Wyatt is the black people's friend and the white people's friend. He ain't scared, and he walks on God's side."

Nancy Jackson called Wyatt "a nice man." She told why: "Mr. Wyatt could be talking nice at the same time he investigatin' you. I got to know him 'cause my first husband would beat up on me, and I had to call Wyatt more than once. One day, he said to me, 'Nancy, the best thing for you to do is to get a divorce because you running like a scared rabbit.' And I did. I got a divorce.

"One night, Wyatt come to my house looking for me. He asked at the door, 'Nancy, here?' My daughter told him I was.

"Wyatt said, 'Y'all got a place for Nancy to stay? Rawleigh has come back.' They were looking for him 'cause he pulled a knife on me. So they took me to the Lampkin's house.

"At 10:00 pm, Wyatt came there and asked if I was there. He said, 'Keep her here 'cause we haven't found Rawleigh yet.' So I stayed there until they found Rawleigh and locked him up."

After her divorce, Jackson married M.K. They were making an adequate living for themselves, in part from their moonshine dealings. One day there was a knock on the door. Nancy was in the kitchen; she wiped her hand on her apron and answered the door. It was the sheriff.

Wyatt sat down on the porch swing and Nancy on a porch chair. "Nancy, how are you and M.K.? Still doing all right?" Wyatt asked, and waited for Nancy's response.

Then he said, "You know, Nancy, I know what's going on here. I see all those cars in your yard on weekends. I know you're doing moonshine.

I haven't arrested you yet 'cause you and M.K. use your money to good purpose like fixing up your house. But if I come by here one day with a deputy in my car, I will have to arrest you."

Nancy was squirming in her chair. Wyatt continued, "You know, there're a lot of folks out here making moonshine, and they're jealous of you and M.K. 'cause you're making more money than they are. But you all don't need the money. M.K. has a good job. You don't need to keep doing this."

Telling the story today, Nancy said, "He talked to me so kind. He talked to me just like a daddy."

"The next somebody that come by for a pint," Nancy said, "I told them, 'I ain't doing no more pints. I'm going out'ta bizness; I'm havin' a sale by the gallons. Then I ain't selling no more.' I wasn't making it; I was jest buying it off the bootlegger and re-selling it.

"So when I sold all the gallons I had hid in the bushes, I never sold the stuff again. I figured I better do what the sheriff said. I knew he wanted the best thing for me, so I did it," Nancy said, looking back.

Nancy told, too, of a black boy who was walking down the road one day acting strange, shouting and throwing rocks at dogs and the cows just to hear the animals holler. Wyatt told his deputies, "Don't shoot; don't hurt him. His mind is not too good."

The integration of the Greene County schools was noted in the Seattle Daily Times. On November 17, 1965, the Times reported that Sheriff Wyatt said four black children began attending classes in Greene County—two in an elementary school in Greensboro and two in an elementary school in Union Point. Sheriff Wyatt stated that there was no trouble. The Rev. A. D. Williams, the pastor of Ebenezer Baptist Church and grandfather of Dr. Martin Luther King, Jr., who spent his early years in Greene County, would have been pleased.

When asked if the black community in Greene County wanted to do a march but were afraid, Vivian Foster, now living in Atlanta said,

"Mr. Wyatt, he was not prejudiced; it's just a first impression you get of a person. He arrested my daddy with his moonshine. He didn't put him in jail, but he said, 'Sid, you know you did wrong; now you pour it all out.' He stood there while my daddy poured out that likker."

More than one black person has said that Wyatt, though he arrested and jailed many black people, treated them as humans. Were they angry about being arrested? "No, he arrested you cause you broke the law," they said.

Shirley Foster, Vivian's sister, related this experience, "One day a man in a black suit and black hat drove up to our house in Siloam. He come up on the porch where my daddy was sitting. He said, 'Sid, yo boys haven't been behaving; your children are missing too many days of Sunday School.' I had nine brothers and they were speeding and doin' the things all teenagers do. And I had four sisters.

"My daddy told the man he would take them uptown to New Springfield Baptist to Sunday School. They talked a while, and then the man walked down the steps toward his car. I was twelve years old. I asked my daddy who that man was.

"My daddy said, 'He's my brother.'

"I'm looking at my daddy and I'm looking at the man getting in that car, and I said to my daddy, 'How can he be your brother? You are black, and he is white.'"

Mr. Foster explained to Shirley that the man was the sheriff, and he was a Mason just like her father was. "And Masons are brothers; they don't go against each other," Foster said.

Shirley said, "I thought Sheriff Wyatt was the nicest white man I ever saw. He was fair, and he treated you like he wished to be treated, and he would do anything for you. He was a true believer in the Lord Jesus Christ just like most Masons."

Years later, a black woman brought an expression of her appreciation for Sheriff Wyatt to Sonny in person. He had retired as a Colonel from the U.S. Army in 1983, and subsequently, from Electronic Data Systems in D.C. in 1999. In 2005, Sonny and his wife, Madeleine, returned to Greene County to live at Reynolds Plantation on Lake Oconee. Sonny developed some medical problems that sent him to Greensboro's Minnie G. Boswell Hospital. One day, he heard a gentle knock on his door.

"Come in," invited Sonny.

In walked a middle-aged black woman. She spoke somewhat apologetically.

"Mr. Sonny, you don't know me, and I don't know you, but my momma knew your daddy, Sheriff Wyatt. That was one good man. My daddy drank a lot, but when my daddy died, the sheriff came to the funeral. Afterward, he sat down with my momma and listened to her for over an hour. He spent more time with her than her minister did. I just had to tell you that my family really appreciated that. We sure did."

Others told Sonny, "Your dad was the only one who listened to me."

The Civil Rights Act passed in 1964. But as far as the blacks of Greene County were concerned, they became equal in the eyes of the sheriff when L.L. Wyatt took office.

Georgia had started out as a free state in which no one could own a slave, and if one were brought in, that slave would be freed. Until the early 1800s, Greene County had the largest number of "Free Persons of Colour" per capita in The United States. That changed with the rise in cotton production and the plantation system, which depended on slaves. After Emancipation, the former slaves in Greene County found themselves often in dire economic circumstances. For some of them, moonshining was a way to survive or get ahead.

103 Year Old Lady
Endorses Sheriff Wyatt

Mrs. Emma Davis, who is 103 years young and the oldest citizen in Greene County, voted for the first time in 1940.

Mrs. Davis stated, "The first man I ever voted for was Sheriff Wyatt and I plan to vote again this year for Sheriff Wyatt."

Mrs. Davis remarked, "Sheriff Wyatt is the black peoples friend and the white peoples friend. He don't judge nobody by the color of their skin but if you break the law he will get you, it don't matter who. He ain't scared and he walks on God's side. I'll keep voting for him the next twenty years if he want it that long."

Mrs. Emma Davis at 103 Years of Age Votes for Wyatt.

15. A Vacation? When?

WYATT RARELY TOOK A VACATION. HE LOVED FAMILY, BUT HE DID not take weekends or evenings off. He did have most of his meals at home with Estelle and Sonny. After Sonny and Madeleine started a family, Wyatt enjoyed seeing them and the grandchildren, Andy, Lee, Jeff, and Cissi, when they were in town. In 1964, Wyatt and Estelle moved from the jail to a home they had built on S. East Street, two blocks from the jail. Even a new home could not keep Wyatt at home. It seemed that Wyatt was everywhere at all times. That perception was part of his effectiveness. But it came at a cost: the cost of seldom, ever having a day off. Though Estelle attended community events with Wyatt, he was at all times on duty. She was often alone but unfailingly supportive.

In 1967, Bobby and Caroline Voyles moved to Greensboro when he was named manager of the (then) Citizens Union Bank. They bought a home on S East Street, too. The Voyleses were in their twenties, and Caroline appreciated having Estelle as a neighbor.

"She took me under her wings," Caroline said. "Estelle would often call to tell me she had something for me. I would go over, and it would be something she had cooked. Often it would be angel biscuits. We loved them. I eventually got her to teach me how to make the biscuits.

I think she was lonely; Wyatt would be coming home late, and she was concerned about him. Estelle was devoted to Wyatt; she worked in the office when they lived at the jail. When they built their home down the street from us, she was thrilled. She was always glad to have Sonny and Madeleine and their children come for a visit."

Periodically, Wyatt would excuse himself from his office, saying, "I'm going out to the country." That announcement was code for going out for target practice. Out in the woods, he could hone his sharp-shooting without anyone watching. He was back at 5:00 p.m. to take down the flag and get home for dinner. After dinner, Wyatt was usually out on the roads again; Wyatt patrolled the back roads of the county day and night.

One evening, sixteen-year-old Perry Underwood was also cruising with three friends, looking for some excitement. Alex, an eighteen-year-old with a car, had suggested they drive down to Flat Rock where he knew some men were gathering to shoot crap. Flat Rock is the largest outcropping of flat granite in Georgia, likely a part of Stone Mountain. The two hundred and fifty-two acres, surrounded by trees, offered a somewhat secluded venue for activities such as picnics by day and gambling by night. Leaving their car on the road, the four young boys crept up quietly toward the flickering fire.

Alex said in a low voice to the gamblers, "Hey, I'm here with some friends."

One of the gamblers said, "Y'all can come on up near the fire to watch. Just stay quiet; we can't 'ford to get distracted." The boys were there for about fifteen minutes.

Suddenly, Perry heard the crunch of footsteps. Perry's body tensed as he turned around to see what was moving toward him. What he saw was a six-foot-tall frame.

It yelled, "Halt! This is Sheriff Wyatt. Nobody run! Nobody move!"

The teenagers froze in place. Wyatt walked over to them, looked into their faces and said, "I caught you, didn't I? This is no place for boys like you on a Friday night. If you boys don't have anything else to do, go home, or you're going to end up in trouble."

As Perry and friends took off, they heard Wyatt ordering the men, "If you folks gonna' do this crap shooting, you go down into the woods all by yourselves. Go back so far that I can't see you 'cause the next time I catch you, I'm gonna' put you in jail."

Another such night, Wyatt parked his car near Flat Rock. He again made his way through the bushes to the dim light in the distance. Wyatt stood a moment in a circle of men. All of a sudden, T. B. Eley, who was dealing, realized he was out of cards and didn't have any left for himself. He had dealt to the feet around the circle. There were nine sets of shoes instead of eight. He could barely see in the dim light.

T.B. blinked his eyes at the size 12 black shoes poking out from under black trousers. He stopped his shuffling cold. He had dealt a hand to Sheriff Wyatt!

"Ah... hello, Sheriff," T.B. said.

Wyatt waved his hand at the group. "You boys go right ahead with your game. I'm not here to raid your game; I'm here to see the Judge."

He and the Judge, a regular at the match, walked out of hearing distance, conferred a few minutes, and then Wyatt was gone.

Bobby Boswell wondered years later how Wyatt knew where that crap game was. "He knew everything that went on in the county; that was the thing about Wyatt. You could not get past him on *anything*," someone reminded Bobby.

Others found they couldn't get past him either. Vivian "Mott" Foster described Wyatt as "cooler than Andy Griffith." It was a rainy Friday night in Georgia when Wyatt arrived at the Grover Kendrick Club in White Plains about twelve miles from Greensboro. The club was packed out, and everybody was having fun. That's when a man in a black raincoat and a "broke-down" hat came through the door and walked up to the front table. He lifted a whiskey glass and poured its contents out onto the concrete floor.

"Then he picked up the next glass and poured it out. He kept on until he had emptied every glass of whiskey at that table. He went from table to table, all around the place, pouring good whiskey out onto the floor,"

Vivian said. The jazz player at the piano had continued to play at first, but then he laid his hands in his lap and waited in the dead silence.

When he had emptied every glass on the premises, the sheriff left. He had not said a word. But he had issued a clear message to the owner: "You have to have a liquor license to sell alcohol." The patrons were left to their tears and their beer. Obtaining a liquor license was not likely to happen in the County Greene, which remained a dry county until five years past Wyatt's time as sheriff. The county went "wet" in 1982, the same year the Lake Oconee resort opened.

Percy Meeks called Wyatt once in the middle of the night for assistance in rescuing a family friend from an alcoholic husband. Two minutes later, Wyatt appeared in his full garb, even the black tie. It was 2:00 a.m.!

Wyatt found Allen Askew and some friends out in the woods at 1:00 a.m. "What you boys doin' out here?" Wyatt asked them.

"We're coon hunting."

"Well, did you find some?"

"Yessir, we got some."

"Well, you boys be careful, now." He left them wondering when he ever slept.

Even Sundays were not sacrosanct if you were the High Sheriff of Greene. Wyatt's diligence and the repeal of the Prohibition Law had knocked the breath out of the moonshine business. By the arrival of the 60s, there wasn't as much going on with 'shine' in Greene County. But neither Wyatt nor dairyman Rooster Boswell was prepared for what *was* going on. At least, not for what Boswell found in his cow pasture one Sunday afternoon.

Rooster was up on a hill overlooking the dairy land behind his house. He spotted a van parked on the dirt road leading to his pasture. Milling around just beyond the van were six young people squatting over something on the ground. Rooster wheeled his truck around and headed down the hill. He pulled his truck up beside the van and jumped out.

Five kids in tie-dyed shirts and jeans with more ragged holes than denim stood up from their stooped positions. The apparent leader wore hair curling around his jawline and braided into a nine-inch ponytail in the back, multiple strings of beads layered over his tie-dyed shirt, and a battered leather hat on his head. A turquoise earring dangled from one ear. He moved into some bends loosely resembling yoga as he stood beside a bucket.

"We're just stretching our legs," he yelled back.

Getting closer, Rooster found that the group was gathering mushrooms. They lifted each mushroom carefully from the cow patties in which they were growing. Boswell hadn't known how valuable his mushrooms were until now.

"Well, this is private property, so I'd appreciate your moving on," Rooster told them.

The bunch complied and piled back into the van. Moments later, Boswell watched as the leader hopped out of the vehicle with a gun. He marched up to Boswell, pointed the gun in his face and began cursing him. Boswell was helpless, his only option to out-stare his enemy. After an eternity, the young man lowered the gun and returned to his van.

There were no cell phones. Rooster high-tailed it up the hill to his shop to call Wyatt. "Hey, Sheriff, I got a bunch of hippies out here invading my property; I need your help."

"I'll be there in four minutes," said Wyatt.

Rooster ran back to his truck. With right hand on the wheel, left hand holding a gun out of the window, and foot on the accelerator, he took off after the van. He was having difficulty shooting at those tires with one hand. Wyatt put out an all-points bulletin, including a request for roadblocks, and arrived to join the chase. Wyatt didn't often lose, but this time, he did not get that Hall County van. The hippies had eluded him.

"What in the world were they stealing my mushrooms *for*?" Rooster asked the sheriff.

The sheriff may have explained that mushrooms growing in cow patties were sometimes brewed into a tea that makes for a real high. Rooster now had another enterprise to add to his dairy.

Occasionally, though, Wyatt managed a day or so away from the job. When he did, Estelle and Wyatt often visited family in Paulding County, where they attended Beulahland Baptist Church. His father, Charles Robert, an active member of the church, sang in the choir, and studied the Bible, often quoting it to his family. He also started the Law and Order Vigilante League to stop the moonshiners. Wyatt's mother, Sarah Emaline Lyle, had a meek and quiet manner. She passed away at forty years of age and soon Charles re-married. Wyatt treated his stepmother with care and respect and after his father died, watched after her.

Wyatt showed the same concern for his siblings: he once drove Estelle and Sonny all the way to Washington, D.C., in 1938 to visit a sister for a few days. Wyatt's brother-in-law was a guard at the White House. It was not a business trip, just family time. They had to use heated bricks in the Ford to stay warm.

Despite his good intentions, when Wyatt did leave, he often returned to trouble. One year, the Wyatt family took a trip to visit a brother in Alabama. They stayed three extra days to take care of some family business. This, one of those few times Wyatt took some time off, caused him to have to dig up a grave when he got home.

WHISKEY STILL CAUGHT

Sheriff L. L. Wyatt, County Policemen Reese Smith, Carlton Lewis examine 100 gallon copper still that was seized in a raid early Thursday morning, near the Daniel Springs Community in Greene County. There were no arrest at the still. Over 300 gallons of mash was destroyed. The still was fixing to run full blast when the officers reached the scene.

Whiskey Still Caught

Lloyd Lee 'Sonny' Wyatt makes Colonel as Major General Vern Bowers does the presentation. Madeleine Wyatt pins the stripes while Andy, Lee, Jeff and Cissi join in the honor.

Name Plate for Wyatt's New Home on S East Street

16. His Day in Court

JUDGE DUKE, KNOWN AS "THE KISSING JUDGE", DIDN'T LIVE IN Greene County. He came in from Milledgeville four times a year to conduct the Superior Court. He liked to make a scene, greeting each woman in the office with a kiss.

The District Attorney was seen by some during court proceedings as a show-off. Wyatt always had the copper spittoon shined up for the tobacco chewing D.A.

In the Superior Courtroom, Wyatt introduced the judge and presided over the court. The judge relied wholly on Wyatt for sentencing. Wyatt knew the circumstances and the people. The judge did not.

Wyatt would say, "Judge, Shook Brown here may be bad, but he's got a good mama and daddy, Uncle Jim Brown and Aunt Maggie. I think you could give Shook a light sentence."

Or he might say, "Judge this is Henry Story; he has six children. If you throw him in jail, no one can provide; a fine would be sufficient."

Wyatt won almost every case he presented. "I tell my deputies to take time, be patient, and when things are strong for you, then you'll get him," Wyatt said to a reporter. "Don't go to court unless you've got a good case."

"I wasn't angry with the sheriff," Eddie Sarden said as he thought about the time Wyatt arrested him, "cause I knew I broke the law. My momma and daddy brought me up with the right frame. Folks need to teach their children to respect the law, and they won't be in so much trouble. But the law needs to treat a person like they are somebody, too. That's what Wyatt did."

Eddie added with a laugh, "We had a sayin' that Wyatt be talking nice and walking you to the jail at the same time!"

While Wyatt and family were in Alabama, he missed a funeral. Back in Greene County, Shag Killiam's house burned with him inside it. The burial had already occurred when Wyatt returned.

Wyatt just didn't feel right about that fire. He did not think the fire killed Killiam. Wyatt's theory was that Shag's grandson, Cecil Brider, had killed his grandfather for his money and then set the house afire. Shag was known for stashing money around in his house.

Wyatt dropped by the coroner's office. "Hey, Bill, you know, I just wonder if that fire killed Shag. I think he was already dead when that house caught fire. I hate to ask you to do this, but I need you to dig up that body and let's take another look."

"Well, you're saying someone killed him before the fire?" questioned Bill.

"Yes," said Wyatt, "I've had dealings with that grandson of his. He's been talking about that cash his grandpa kept stashed around the house. I'm going over to talk to him." Folks who knew Killiam knew that he did not have a bank account but kept $300-$400 in cash in various places throughout his house.

"Okay, I'll have it dug up this afternoon, and we can take another look." Bill knew his business, but he now was as interested as Wyatt in taking a second look.

At the opening of the casket were the coroner, the newspaper editor with his camera, and Wyatt. Wyatt was right again. There on the back of Killiam's head and difficult to see under the burns, was a sunken spot. It appeared he had been killed by blunt force before the fire. Brider was sentenced to five years in prison.

All of Wyatt's big cases seem to have happened in December. During Christmas holidays of 1958, the much loved and respected Greensboro High School principal, Roy Burke, went missing. He had gone fishing with a friend at Clarke Hill Dam but had not returned. Burke let his friend out at one location to get into a different boat. The friend never saw Burke again. He did not show at the rendezvous spot at the end of the day, and the friend could not locate Burke on the waters. He called Wyatt.

Wyatt and Prince Parrish organized search teams to dredge the lake. They dredged in the cold winter waters for 29 days. Wyatt came out in a small fishing boat one day to join the search party in Prince's larger vessel. Just as the sheriff stepped into their boat, one of the volunteers was taking a swig of moonshine.

"Oh, my goodness... sorry, Sheriff; I'm just trying to stay warm," he said as he wiped his mouth with his sleeve.

Wyatt responded, "That's all right, fellows, we're trying to do something good here."

Burke was found floating under his boat at the bottom of the lake. The boat had capsized when its propeller caught in some old dredging net in the lake. The boat with Burke under it had sunk to the bottom of the lake.

In December of 1975, Wyatt investigated the high profile and brutal murder case of Reuben Flynt, vice-president of the Farmers Bank of Union Point. Two men had gone to Flynt's home while he was there alone for lunch and murdered him, gaining access to his billfold.

They arrived back at the bank in a late model car. One of them entered the bank, and showed the teller the wallet.

"The man who gave me this said he has Reuben Flynt. Give me $60,000 in 15 minutes or he'll be dead," the man said in an extortion attempt.

Joanne Newsome Cathy was leaving for lunch when she heard the robber's demand. Because he was not looking her way, she stopped to listen and realized that the billfold was actually that of Mr. Flynt. She quietly slipped back into her office in the bank and informed her co-workers what was going on. "What should I do?" she asked. They suggested she notify someone, so she called Wayne Jackson at City Hall. He summoned help. Wyatt and Deputy Smith, hearing the news on the police radio, headed to Union Point.

As the robber exited the bank with the money, Union Point Police Chief Carlton Lewis, alerted by the bank's alarm system, arrived and arrested the man. Seeing his friend drop the bags of money, the second man, waiting in the parked car, fled the scene.

Investigating the case, Sheriff Wyatt described a murder in which Flynt was shot four times with a .22 caliber pistol and beaten with the butt end of a gun. Just the evening before, Flynt had stood at the door of the bank greeting each person as the employees arrived for their annual Christmas Party. He was much loved and respected in Union Point and throughout the county.

Someone identified the fleeing suspect as Charlie Young. Wyatt went straight to the nearby home of the suspect's grandmother. There sat the murderer in his bloody clothes, having his lunch. While law enforcement surrounded the house, Young surrendered without resistance. Wyatt arrested him and took him to jail. The other suspect, arrested at the bank, was his cousin, Derwin Young. Five hundred folks crowded into the courthouse square in Greensboro when the two were being questioned in separate rooms.

Cathy later testified at the trial that she had seen the young man two weeks earlier to the day walking around in the parking lot of the bank. When he saw her, he hopped into his vehicle and took off. She wondered if she should have said something then. It was reported that a car dealer in Morgan County said that two weeks before, the would-be extortionist had bought a sports car, stating, "You don't need any references or anything because I will be back in two weeks with cash for the whole thing."

Wyatt said of Flynt, "He was a mighty fine citizen, a good banker, one of our best." The horrific event was headlined in newspapers across the country.

After 28 years as a model prisoner and three execution dates stayed, Charlie was released on a technicality. He became a Christian while in prison and tells his story to at-risk groups, hoping to help them make better choices than he previously did. Derwin was released in 1986 after serving 11 years. He had not been involved in the murder, but had remained in the car while it was happening. He was the one entering the bank with the billfold.

In December 1974, at 70 years of age, Wyatt faced the biggest challenge of his career.

Wyatt Investigates a Crime Scene with Jim Duff and Donna Hazelip of Georgia Crime Lab. No murder went unsolved while Wyatt was Sheriff.

17. Grabbing National Headlines

WYATT TOOK HIS USUAL STROLL DOWN TO THE POST OFFICE FOR the morning mail. It was December 18, 1974. Wyatt walked back up Main Street, admiring the Christmas decorations in the store windows and on the streetlights. He was kept busy tipping his hat to the ladies who were out in full force to get their Christmas shopping done. He was probably thinking about Sonny and Madeleine and the grandchildren, wishing they could be in Greensboro with Estelle and him for Christmas. This close to Christmas, a sheriff tended to regret the times his job interrupted family Christmas celebrations.

But, folks go wild around this time of year, Wyatt might have thought as he walked back to the courthouse. *Money pressures just cause folks to do some crazy things.* Every year, he hoped it would be different, but it never was.

In mid-afternoon, Wyatt returned to his office from a chat with Judge Brown. He was just settling into his chair when Carey Williams from *The Herald Journal* popped in. At the same time, Wyatt's police radio crackled. "All points alert: Police have been called to the State Bank of Wrens, Georgia, where a robbery is taking place. Police already on the scene report three robbers are in the bank where a blistering exchange of gunfire is taking place between one officer and the robbers...we are told that a teller has been shot in the hail of bullets. She has fallen to the floor. Doesn't look good..."

Williams looked at Wyatt. "Sounds big, doesn't it?" Wyatt agreed.

Wyatt called his pastor, Rev. Harold Tice, to join them in listening to the reports. Tice had pastored in Wrens before coming to Greensboro and might know the hostages. Wyatt sat, pondering what might happen. The attention of the three was glued to the radio.

The radio crackled again: "We are told that one robber has emptied his revolver at police and has fled through the front door of the bank. The two other robbers are moving toward the back exit, each taking a hostage with them. The officers are attempting to shoot without harming the hostages." Silence. "The robbers are demanding a getaway car. We'll see what transpires from here."

Sheriff Compton in Wrens kept stalling for time to close all exits out of the town. The robbers were losing patience, threatening to kill one by one the eleven hostages spread-eagle on the floor of the bank vault. *O Little Town of Bethlehem* playing over the bank's public address system seemed to make the robbers edgier. Eugenia Braswell, in the grasp of Lee Houston, talked to the sheriff for the fifth time and pleaded with him to bring the car. Compton agreed to the car after he spoke with Houston, getting his pledge to release the hostages once they were out of town.

The 1972 white Ford arrived at the drive-in booth. The robbers, each tightly covered by a hostage, made their way to the car. The sharpshooters on the roof of the bank could see no way to take out the robbers without harming their hostages. Larry Dorsey backed into the rear seat holding Barbara Prescott for cover while Houston slid into the front seat with Braswell as cover. Houston, with a gun to Braswell's head, directed her to drive GA 17 to Thomson where they would take I-20/West to Atlanta. Dorsey lifted his gun to Prescott seated beside him and holding the sack of money.

As the getaway car sped down Main Street in Wrens, they faced a roadblock. Houston shouted that he was going to kill Braswell if they didn't move the barrier. The police opened up the block.

State troopers followed the chase from the bank, giving reports as the bandits' car made its way out of Wrens, through a red light at the heart of Stapleton and onto GA 17, headed toward Interstate 20. A gathering procession of over 50 vehicles roared after the robbers. In the chase were the Georgia Bureau of Investigation, the Federal Bureau of Investigation, the State Patrol, local police, and sheriffs from nearby counties.

The all points alert announced: "State Troopers are following Wrens, Georgia, bank robbers headed toward I-20 near Thomson. Two robbers, armed and dangerous, holding two hostages, one hostage driving the white 1972 Ford. The vehicle is being followed by over 50 patrol cars in the chase from Wrens. They are being tracked via helicopter along the way."

Occasionally there was the crackle of the radio with the troopers in the chopper instructing the patrol cars following the getaway car, "Drop back... they may release those hostages."

Wyatt listened intently to the updates, predicting what might occur.

All points alert: "State Troopers are following Wrens Georgia Bank Robbers turning west onto I-20 at Thomson. Headed toward Atlanta at 100 mph. Two robbers, armed and dangerous, and holding two hostages, one hostage driving the white 1972 Ford. A third bank employee is dead at the scene of the robbery."

Wyatt raised his voice. "Do you hear that? Wonder what the troopers are going to do."

Turning to Tice, Wyatt said, "They're headed our way; let's ride out there." He picked up Fire Chief Omer Cook, Jr., and went by his home for another weapon. Williams went to his office for his camera.

Just twenty minutes later, their nerves went on high alert as the radio crackled again: "State Troopers here in the helicopter overhead. We've been following the chase up U.S. 278/ I-20. They are traveling at a speed of 100 miles per hour. This is a blanket request for a roadblock to be set up at the Union Point/Siloam Exit 138 in Greene County."

Sheriff Wyatt, Rev. Tice, and Fire Chief Omer Cook Jr. left in the sheriff's car, heading to the I-20 Exit at Siloam, only seven miles away. Once he reached the exit, Wyatt placed his car in the middle of westbound I-20. He instructed Tice and Cook to begin flagging down trucks.

Truckers seemed happy to be a part of the razor-edged excitement. In a matter of minutes, three large trucks blocked the two lanes westbound. A tractor-trailer rig was placed across the 138 Exit ramp. Other unmarked police cars joined Wyatt at the overpass.

The arrival of the police helicopter and the press plane from the east meant that the getaway car was right beneath it. When the bandits came around the curve, Houston placed the gun to Braswell's head and ordered her to go through the roadblock. Dorsey put his gun to Prescott's head saying he would kill her if they didn't make the ramp.

Braswell quickly maneuvered the vehicle, zigzagging around the tractor-trailer rig blocking the exit and up across a grassy field and back to the exit ramp. At the top of the ramp, the car made an abrupt right turn onto Highway 77 toward Union Point and ultimately US 278 to Atlanta.

"Oh, hell," crackled state troopers on Wyatt's radio, "they're entering L.L. Wyatt territory now; this ain't gonna' be good."

At that, Wyatt rushed to his car, working out a plan in his mind as he went. The ever-growing entourage of vehicles moved in sync as the chase took them at top speed around the curves and up and down the hills of State 77 behind the getaway car. Wyatt did not join them. He and his riders drove at a speed of over 120 miles per hour back I-20 to Greensboro and over to U.S. 278, to ready the path the getaway car was sure to take to Atlanta.

As Wyatt reached Greensboro, his police broadcast blared. "The bank robbers are leaving Union Point heading towards Greensboro on U.S. 278."

Just outside of Greensboro, toward Union Point, Wyatt selected the spot for his roadblock. This time, the spot, at the bottom of a hill, was flanked by trees on one side, a body of water on the other, and deep ditches on both sides. It was a perfect trap.

At the dip in U.S Highway 278, Wyatt parked his black Ford across the middle of the highway. He then had the City of Greensboro Police Car, and a deputy sheriff's car placed on each side of his, entirely blocking the road. On this occasion, Wyatt had his pistol on his person.

The moments had grown tense as the getaway car covered the six miles to Union Point at 110 mph. The helicopter hovered overhead all the way. Over 60 patrol cars now trailed the getaway car. As they reached U.S. Highway 278 in Union Point, the robbers burned the rubber in a screeching left turn onto 278 and headed straight toward the roadblock four miles ahead.

Carey Williams Jr. was up front at the scene with his camera. Reese Smith, a deputy, was strategically placed on the right side of Wyatt's car with Deputy Carlton Lewis on the other.

From inside their homes, nearby neighbors realized something big was going on as they watched the helicopter sputtering their way—directly over the Union Point-Greensboro Highway. Comer Tolbert walked out to see the helicopter as it circled over the Greensboro Post Office where he worked and then moved back over toward the Chevrolet Place near today's Ingles Grocery. He wondered what in the world was going on. Judge Ogletree was at work in the probate office at the courthouse. She, too, wondered what was going down in Greensboro that had brought in a helicopter.

Roberta Smith, the wife of Deputy Reese Smith, saw one patrol car after another whizzing by her as she drove east to appointments in Washington, Georgia. She had never seen that many patrol cars in Greene County.

Two hours after leaving the Wrens bank, the robber/gunmen were upon the Wyatt roadblock, surrounded by a wall of police cars and state troopers, with nowhere to go. The gunmen were angry, cursing each other, but they held their guns. Dorsey, in the back seat, held his .38 caliber on the hostage seated beside him. Houston in the front held his .20 gauge sawed-off shotgun at the temple of the driver/hostage. The folks of Greene County held their breaths.

Braswell, the driver/hostage, scared for her very life, screamed out the window, "Let us through! Please, let us through; he's going to kill me if you don't!"

Sheriff Wyatt jumped out of his car and walked toward the white Ford as it continued to move forward. Standing squarely in front of the car, Wyatt held his hand up toward Union Point, signaling, "Stop!" His other hand grasped his pistol. Everyone gasped at his courage. Wyatt was allowing himself to become a human decoy to save the hostages. More than at any other time, his audience held onto their belief that Wyatt could handle anything, even this. Rev. Tice, with head bowed, prayed for the hostages, for Wyatt, and, yes, for the robbers.

In the front seat, the gunman panicked and turned his sawed-off shotgun from the hostage to the approaching Sheriff. He pulled the trigger. Wyatt heard it click. The gun misfired. *Who was praying harder—the sheriff or the pastor?* Wyatt was then right on the car. He fired through the windshield. Deputy Reese Smith shot twice with a deer rifle. Bank robber Lee Houston was dead.

Carey Williams, there to take photographs, said of Wyatt, "He was right on him when he fired."

"Mrs. Eugenia Braswell was driving the car when it stopped," Williams said. "The sheriff jumped out in front of it and pointed his pistol right at the windshield. He was right on top of them."

Braswell received minor cuts from flying glass as the sheriff's gunfire tore through the windshield, but she rolled to safety in a nearby ditch.

As he went to the aid of the freed hostage, Rev. Tice was stunned to discover she was Eugenia Braswell, organist of the church he had pastored in Wrens. She later said to a reporter that she "kept thinking as I drove along that I'd never see my family again. And I kept thinking that I had the junior choir practice at church that night and I wouldn't be back in time."

The second gunman, Larry Dorsey, wounded in the shootout, threw his .38 caliber pistol out the door and surrendered. "Don't shoot; he's unarmed," called Wyatt to the camp of officers moving in toward the car. Wyatt arrested Dorsey. Barbara Prescott, the other hostage, was rescued from the back seat, unharmed, but sobbing from the trauma of it all. Rev. Tice now sought to comfort Prescott.

Suddenly, Wyatt was stampeded by friends, sheriffs from neighboring counties, and state patrolmen congratulating him. State Trooper Dimeno found his way through the crowd to Wyatt, presenting him Houston's sawed-off shotgun and the shell that had been in it when Houston pulled the trigger. The shell showed that the firing pin had struck the primer, but the gun did not go off.

"The Lord was protecting me," said Wyatt, "just as He has all these years."

"Yeah, but this time, He was *really* looking out for you," Dimeno said.

Police swarmed the area while $25,000 dollars of stolen cash was removed from the car.

Roberta Smith, driving back from Washington, came upon the roadblock and the horde of police cars on the Union Point/Greensboro Highway. She couldn't get through. She got out of her car. The patrol ordered her to get back into her car. "Someone has been hurt," they told her.

"Well," said Smith, "I need to check on my husband; he's a deputy with Sheriff Wyatt."

"It wasn't any law enforcement people; it was a bank robber that was shot," the patrol assured her.

As soon as she could get through the blockade, Roberta rushed home. In the kitchen stood her husband, his face white as a sheet, his body bent over the sink, his hands trembling as he tried to drink a glass of water. Smith had never seen her husband look like this. "What happened?" Roberta asked Reese.

"I shot the robber," he answered. He never spoke of the incident again. Sheriff Wyatt had put his life on the line for the hostages. And his Deputy Smith had backed him up.

The third gunman, Julius Rauls, had escaped from the scene of the crime but was found later hiding in a motel in Warrenton, Georgia. He had been seriously injured by the officers' gunfire as he was leaving the bank. Motel employees reported his whereabouts, and authorities transported him to a hospital for treatment. Staff found sheets soaked in blood in the bathroom of the room where he had lodged. Linda Lamb, a bank employee, was shot during the robbery by a bullet believed to be from Dorsey's gun. The robbers' delay caused Lamb to die before medical help reached her.

In an interview on Dec. 19, the day after the shoot-out, Wyatt reflected, "As soon as I had a chance, I fired. The only thing I was concerned about was those hostages."

Wyatt said he began walking toward the car and could see a man holding a shotgun to Mrs. Braswell's head.

"I just kept walking. The man took the shotgun off the hostage and pointed it at me. I could hear the hammer click. I let him have it through the windshield," said Wyatt. "He turned for an instant and pointed his gun at me. That gave me my chance. We hit the trigger at the same time. My gun fired," said Wyatt. "His didn't."

Later, Wyatt, holding the shotgun with gingerness, said, "This gun could've taken my life." His head was bowed in reverence, not for the gun, but for God, who protected him from it. The sawed-off shotgun hangs today in a framed case with other Wyatt memorabilia in the

Wyatt Museum at the Administration Building of the Greene County Sheriff's Headquarters.

Braswell, the driver hostage, said after her rescue, "I just knew I was going to die, but I did not want it in the head with that shotgun."

Someone described the scene, "It just wasn't real. There were about 60 or 70 cars behind us with their sirens going, there were these armed men flanking us, and there was this helicopter right over us. But this man didn't seem aware of any of it. He just kept walking into that shotgun."

"I knew we weren't going any further when Wyatt approached the car and fired," Braswell said as she reflected further on the day.

Sonny Wyatt, a colonel in the U. S. Army, heard the news of his father's heroic action over the American Forces Network in Germany. He was not a bit surprised but still amazed at his daring. Madeleine, living back in Virginia with their children, learned about the bravery when friends began calling and asking, "Is that Sonny's father they're talking about on the news?" Madeleine flipped on her TV and saw her father-in-law on the national news.

In Germany, Sonny picked up the phone and called his father. "What in the hell do you think you're doing? You're too darned old to do something like that," chided Sonny, though he was bursting with pride for his father.

Wyatt answered, "Just doing my job, son, just doing my job." Wyatt did not speak about the event the next day in the office. He did not look at shooting someone as something to be celebrated. Perhaps, too, he was still processing how close to death he had been.

But reporters called in from all over the country. The news hit all the major newspapers and radio and television news channels. Overnight, Wyatt and Greene County with him were catapulted into the national spotlight. A sampling of headlines on December 19, 1974, and days following, read:

"Bandit Killed by Shot Through Windshield"
— The Cincinnati Inquirer

"Photo of GA's Oldest Sheriff With Sawed-Off Shotgun"
— State Times, Baton Rouge

"Sheriff Kills Robbery Suspect With Hostages at Roadblock"
— Sarasota Herald-Tribune

"Lawmen Recount Chase of Robbery Suspects"
—Augusta Chronicle, Dec 20, 1974

"Septuagenarian Sheriff Stops, Slays Suspect"
— Florence Morning News

"Sheriff's Marksmanship Ends 100-mile Chase"
—News-Herald, Panama City, FL

When asked later what moves a man to walk into such danger, Wyatt reflected again, "It's my job. That's what I was sworn to do when I took the oath of office. You don't think of being afraid; you can't afford to. If you permit yourself to think about danger, you might do something wrong. I'm living on borrowed time anyway."

Though Wyatt saw the event as "just another day" in law enforcement, he did not take lightly having to shoot someone. "We hate to see anyone killed," Wyatt said. "We try to do our job without resorting to violence. But the choice is actually up to those who break the law. When a man comes at you shooting, he doesn't leave you a whole lot of choice."

On October 13, 1975, L.L. Wyatt was awarded the Georgia Peace Officer of the Year Award, fifty years from the date he began in Greene County. The award was given by the 10,000 members of the Peace Officers Association of Georgia whose membership is composed of sheriffs, city police, state patrol, county police, solicitors, correctional officers, revenue agents, rangers, and F.B.I. agents. From 1925 to 1940, police officer Wyatt rid Greene County of bootleggers. From 1941—1977, Sheriff Wyatt gave Greene the reputation of one of Georgia's most crime-free areas.

Wyatt was one of few honored, too, with a lifetime membership in the GA Peace Officer Association. In nominating Wyatt, Captain L. F. Butler stated, "He is a very quiet and conservative man who with his wife has made a great contribution and has set an example for Law Enforcement Officers now and in the future. His life is an open book for anyone to inspect."

The guns and the headlines of Wyatt's heroics in saving two hostages from Wrens, GA. bank robbers. Wyatt states "I'm living on borrowed time, anyway."

18. Hollywood Comes A Calling

THE WRENS BANK ROBBERY INCIDENT CAUGHT THE ATTENTION OF Hollywood. Screenwriter Buddy Atkinson of *The Beverly Hillbillies* fame spent months in Greensboro collecting stories and shadowing Wyatt in his duties. Atkinson had been sent by the actor John Wayne's movie production company to write the story of Wyatt, from which a film later could be made. Wyatt gave his permission to the John Wayne Company for the proposed book and movie. The High Sheriff had made his people proud once again.

Interestingly, the sheriff's son, Lloyd L., had already been in a film, the 1955 Hollywood movie *To Hell and Back* with Audie Murphie. Lloyd L. "Sonny" had played "Pierce," a Tank Commander, in an un-credited role. The movie was filmed at Fort Lewis and other locations in Washington state.

The folks in Greene County liked Buddy Atkinson. Atkinson grew up in neighboring Morgan County. He had heard stories of Wyatt before the sheriff hit national headlines. He probably had little difficulty envisioning Wyatt's charisma and courage in a Hollywood thriller.

Atkinson spent a total of eighteen months in the County Greene with Wyatt and those who had stories to tell about him. Judge Ogletree could overhear Atkinson trying to pry information out of Wyatt. Even with Atkinson's screenwriting skills, he was finding it difficult to get into Quiet Wyatt's psyche.

Commenting on his time with Wyatt, Atkinson said in *The Herald Journal,* "People today are more law and order conscious than ever before.

I never have read or heard of a police officer that has had the experiences over such a distinguished career as Greene County Sheriff L.L. Wyatt. In the short time, I have known him, I have learned to respect him highly as everyone that knows him does…"

During this time, Wyatt took his deputy, Reese Smith, and his administrative assistant, Jan Gentry, to the last operating moonshine still in Greene County. The year was 1977. With Wyatt and Gentry looking on, Smith ceremoniously took an ax and chopped up the still. The moonshine days of Greene County were over. At least for now. The sheriff did not think of making it a photo op. The drama would have made a fitting scene in Atkinsons' proposed movie of "the man in black."

An unforeseen event lurking in the shadows brought Atkinson's plans to a standstill.

Sheriff and Mrs. Wyatt at home

19. A Bad Good Friday in the County Greene

"I CAN'T BELIEVE THEY HAVEN'T CUT THE GRASS. AND IT'S EASTER Weekend!" Wyatt said as he looked out across the courthouse lawn. "I'm going out there and mow it because we're likely to have visitors in town this weekend."

"One of the deputies can do it; you don't have to," Jan Gentry told him.

"Oh, no, I don't mind," Wyatt answered. "I'll get it done and then go to lunch."

The temperature was a humid 87 degrees that morning of April 8, 1977. But Wyatt pushed the hand-powered lawn mower back and forth across the one-acre lawn until the grass was to his liking. Then he walked to his car on Court Street, drove two blocks to his home on East Street, and pulled his car into the drive. Wyatt opened the back door to his home, walked into the mudroom, and splashed his face with the cool water.

Then he fell over, dead of an apparent heart attack. What no shot had done to the High Sheriff of Greene, the intensity of the job did. He had, in fact, spent his last morning in conference on a particularly disturbing rape case in which a minor had been victimized by an 89 year old. The county was paralyzed. The high sheriff of Greene — *their* Mr. Sheriff — was now gone. Magistrate Court Judge Brown, in his office next to Wyatt's, shook his head in disbelief. "This has created a void we'll *never* fill."

Joel McCray, the owner of the Greensboro Florist, said, "His death saddened the whole county and state. We all felt a paragon of righteousness was gone."

In Virginia, Wyatt's grandchildren arrived home from school to find their daddy already home and their suitcases packed. Sonny gathered them around and said, "Your grandfather has had a heart attack and died at home—in the mudroom." They soon left for Greensboro.

Close friends began to gather at the Wyatt home to be with Estelle and to bring food. One of those was Nancy Webb, now a 21-year-old college student, saddened and heartbroken at the loss of her friend and mentor. Estelle asked her to join them for lunch and to give the prayer before the meal. Nancy remembered, "I was deeply moved that she asked me to pray. I found the telephone book and scribbled my prayer in the back in the yellow pages as I was very unsure I could make it through the prayer. I tore it out and held it while I prayed. I still have the scribbled prayer and a beautiful memory of the man that saw potential in me and helped change my life."

Here is Nancy's prayer: "Our Heavenly Father, look down on this home today with love and comfort these loved ones. Bless Miss Estelle and give comfort in this hour of sorrow. Let us give thanks for knowing such a fine man and now let us carry forth in a manner pleasing to you and to him... Amen."

Though it was the Friday before Easter, it was not a good Friday in the County Greene.

20. The People Wept

IT WAS ONE OF THE LARGEST FUNERALS EVER IN THE COUNTY. THE florist shop in Greensboro sold out. Joel McCray filled orders until the time of the burial at the cemetery. It seemed that every county police department, every sheriff's department, every statewide law enforcement organization and politicians sent flowers, as did a host of local citizens.

The funeral service was held on Easter Sunday, April 10th at the First Baptist Church in Greensboro. Even standing room was filled. The Rev. E.A. Kilgore, the Rev. Harold Tice, and the Rev. Jimmy Waters officiated. The order of service is not known since no copy of the printed program is available. Most who were present have hazy memories of the service as they were all in a state of shock and disbelief.

The Evans Bible Class served as pallbearers. Honorary pallbearers were deputies Reese Smith, Mike Richardson, Jimmy Finch, Fred Webb, Union Point Police Chief Carlton Lewis, and Game Warden Charles Copelan. A flag draped the coffin as a symbol of honor for his service to his people.

The Rev. Jimmy Waters, pastor of Mabel White Memorial Baptist Church, Macon, and chaplain of GA Peace Officers Association, pronounced the graveside eulogy. An honor guard of the Sheriff's Association gave a salute and the presentation of the flag to Estelle.

Jimmy Waters said it well: "Today we bury a living legend. A man who was respected by all walks of life. His word was his bond. When it came to being a police officer, Sheriff L. L. Wyatt of Greene County was the best. He was second to none who ever pinned on the badge."

And the people wept.

Condolences came in from everywhere, from notables such as Senator Sam Nunn and Governor George Busbee.

Senator Sam Nunn wrote, "He represented the finest tradition in the field of law enforcement and was recognized as one of the outstanding law enforcement officials in the nation. Although Georgia has lost one of its finest, Sheriff Wyatt's exemplary record of service will be a lasting tribute to him."

Governor George Busbee wrote, "Sheriff Wyatt was loved and respected by all. His knowledge of and dedication to law enforcement will long be felt by the citizens of Georgia."

On Saturday, the day before the funeral, people had come from all over Georgia to pay their respects at the McCommons Funeral Home where the body lay in repose for public viewing. Many who came did not even know Sheriff Wyatt but had heard of him and respected him. Hundreds in the county, who loved and respected him, came to pay their tribute to one whose leadership had kept them free of racial trouble and made the county one of the most crime-free in Georgia, perhaps the country.

While hundreds were showing their respect to Wyatt, one man was conscientiously preparing the resting place for the High Sheriff. The tale about this gravedigger is still around today.

The story is that Bill McCommons had a gravedigger named Turner Jackson.

McCommons always worried that the gravedigger finished too early and maybe the grave would not be deep enough. The day before Wyatt's funeral, however, Turner was at the cemetery for at least an hour longer than usual. McCommons decided to drive out to the cemetery to see what was going on. He found Turner still down in the grave, digging.

McCommons called down, "Turner, what's taking you so long?"

Turner, wiping the sweat from his forehead, yelled back up, "You did say this here grave belongs to the sheriff, didn't you?"

"Yes, I did," McCommons answered, squatting to look down into the grave.

"Well," Turner shouted, "I jest want to be sure that man don't ever get outta' this grave!"

There seemed to be a *few* people who were glad he was dead! Wyatt was hated by few, revered by many, and respected by all.

United States Senate
WASHINGTON, D. C. 20510

SAM NUNN
GEORGIA

May 4, 1977

Dear Mrs. Wyatt:

  I was deeply saddened to learn of Sheriff Wyatt's death. He was a good friend and supporter of mine and I will always cherish the memory of our friendship. My thoughts and prayers are with you and your family during this time of sorrow.

  Throughout his 52 years of dedicated service, Sheriff Wyatt inspired respect and admiration in all those fortunate enough to work with him. He represented the finest tradition in the field of law enforcement and was recognized as one of the outstanding law enforcement officials in the nation.

  Although Georgia has lost "one of its finest," Sheriff Wyatt's exemplary record of service will be a lasting tribute to him.

Sincerely,

Sam Nunn

Mrs. Estell B. Wyatt
East Street
Greensboro, Georgia 30642

Letter of Condolence from Senator Sam Nunn

Office of the Governor
Atlanta, Georgia 30334

George Busbee
GOVERNOR

April 8, 1977

Mrs. L. L. Wyatt
East Street
Greensboro, Georgia 30642

Dear Mrs. Wyatt:

The news of your husband's death reached me this
afternoon and I was extremely saddened to learn of
your great loss.

Sheriff Wyatt was loved and respected by all. His
knowledge of and dedication to law enforcement will
long be felt by the citizens of Georgia.

To you and your family, I wish to extend my very
deepest sympathy.

Sincerely,

George Busbee
George Busbee

GB/da

Letter of Condolence from Governor Busbee

1904 — 1977

"Second to None!"

21. The Opening of the Till

WYATT WAS ALWAYS JINGLING CHANGE IN HIS POCKETS. OR SHUF-fling it from one hand to another as he talked. His grandchildren told of his giving them money when they visited.

Before going to the hardware store, Wyatt once gave the three grandsons, Andy, Lee, and Jeff, several dollar bills each, and he gave a pocketful of coins to their younger sister. The granddaughter, Cissi, saw that hers was not the same and plaintively said to her grandfather, "I want some *big* money, too."

The bank manager remembered Wyatt's bringing the four grandchildren to the bank and showing them stacks of money. "Which stack is mine?" one of them asked.

It is said that Wyatt refused to buy a cup of coffee at the drugstore after it went above five cents a cup. He never spent money on himself except for his cars and his weekly haircut. Though Wyatt did pay cash for the home he finally had built, his reputation for frugality was obvious as he questioned every dime that was spent.

Though he was a bank director, Wyatt had no savings account, only a till which he rented at the bank. In that till were his life's savings, savings accumulated from his fees and his frugal lifestyle, sitting in a vault gaining no interest. When they opened the till after his death, the bank and the family were absolutely stunned. Now the grandchildren could ask, "Which *stacks* are mine?"

Wyatt was one of the last sheriffs in Georgia to be paid solely on the fee system. Sheriffs received one-third of every fee collected. The district attorneys were also on the fee system. Out of their fees, sheriffs had to pay their deputies, purchase their cars and pay for the upkeep, and care for the prisoners, including their food, bedding, and sometimes their clothing. Estelle and the sheriff made sure the prisoners of Greene County were taken care of and their families as well. And for the first time in the history of the jail, the prisoners had sheets on the beds and ate the same food as the jailers.

In the 19th century and early 20th century, sheriffs were paid solely by the fees collected from the functions they performed. In 1959, the Georgia General Assembly ended the fee system, putting all sheriffs on salary. It took some time for all counties to change over to the salary system. Wyatt changed over to the salary system for his last four years, beginning in 1973.

22. Could the High Sheriff of Greene Do It Today?

SOME IN GREENSBORO TODAY BELIEVE HE COULD IN A FERGUSON, Missouri, or a Hattiesburg, Mississippi, or a New York City. Wyatt could walk into a situation and, just by his cool disposition, disperse a crowd. It takes a person who has control of himself and his emotions. It takes treating others as you want to be treated. It takes the ability to try to talk them through it. But if they cross a certain line, there is no coming back. "Listen to your people; get to know them," Wyatt might say. He was a community policeman and sheriff before there was one.

"We don't know how many he steered out of jail because you knew if you crossed him you would end up under the jail," said Sonny Wyatt.

Bobby Voyles agreed. "I would say that perhaps his greatest work is the number of folks he kept *out* of jail."

Joel McCray saw Wyatt's crime prevention program this way: "Wyatt was so intense in doing his job that he intimidated folks before they tried things. 'No need to try that because Wyatt would find you out.' At the same time, I would describe him with a word not generally associated with someone of his stature or of someone in law enforcement. The word that keeps coming to me when I think of Wyatt is 'genteel.'" *Polite, well-mannered, decorous, free of vulgarity or rudeness while enforcing the law?* Imagine it!

Wyatt might have to carry a gun today, and he might have to use handcuffs. He might have to wear body armor, and he might have to wear a camera. He might have to shoot more often. But he would first try to talk people down; he would show the respect of listening; he would say, "Come with me, now, before one of us gets hurt."

The changing world made Wyatt uneasy as he witnessed the rise in drugs and violence. "I've got to protect my people," Sonny remembered his father's saying more than once as he reflected on the changes, "and you have to have law enforcement behind you to do it." Today Wyatt might add that you have to have the community behind law enforcement.

Wyatt would make an exemplary community police officer or sheriff today. He would build community informants by tirelessly getting to know the people. He would garner new respect for the law by the manner in which he enforced it. He would be tenacious in steering youth away from the gangs and the drugs. He would dissolve the war between the law and the citizens who feel disenfranchised by showing how the law is for their good. He would reach across the color divide by relating to all with respect. In his gentility, he would treat each person as if they were "one of my people!"

In knowing the people, Wyatt could prevent crime today rather than just responding after a crime has been committed. In the major cities, he would have to train his deputies to get out of their cars, go to neighborhood meetings and events. Even funerals. Be seen where non-profits are developing young men and women for careers rather than a life of crime. He would have to create a reputation for that delicate balance of respect for the person *and* the law. This is difficult if a culture allows an anti-cop atmosphere to grow and seed itself.

In short, Wyatt's epic qualities of bravery, corporeal strength, self-control, and fearlessness, reinforced by a sense of divine calling and a belief that God would protect him, could do it today. A hero can be afraid; he just can't allow it to take control.

A sheriff, following in Wyatt's wake in 2015, said of the sheriff's office in Greene County, "I believe I am a public servant… and the people who work with me are public servants. They (the public) do not serve us. We want to reach out to the community because we are only as good as the information we're sometimes given… We want people to trust us and to know that we are going to do the best job we can for them. I'm going to be accessible and available to the people of this county."

Since no one can easily follow a legend, it took the county twenty years and four sheriffs to 'straighten out' the vacuum left by Wyatt's death. Here are the requirements for being a sheriff, in the words of L.L. Wyatt himself:

> Honesty is the first requirement. Being honest with yourself and everybody goes a long way.
>
> Second, you have to treat everyone like you would want to be treated.
>
> Third, it helps to have an attentive ear. Most people who come to you have lots of problems that may seem small to you, but the problems are big to them. So it pays to do a lot of listening.
>
> Fourth, you need to use your best judgment all the time, though sometimes, you'll go wrong.
>
> Finally , you need the patience of Job and a skin as thick as I don't know what.

23. Wyattisms

THIS SHORT CHAPTER GIVES WISDOM FROM WYATT QUOTED BY those who worked closely with him. The quotes are illustrative of the Wyatt described in the previous chapters.

"You can spend a lifetime building a good reputation
and do one bad deed and blow it."
—L. G. Boswell

"You never fail to ask for the vote."
—Jan Gentry

"You cannot control how people act or feel toward you, but you can
control how you deal with other people."
—Nancy Jacobs

"Don't ever sign a petition because if you want to run for office, it'll
come back to haunt you."
—Jan Gentry

"Whatever you do, do it well."
—Lloyd Lee "Sonny" Wyatt

"If it's not the truth, I'll have no part of it."
—Lloyd Lee "Sonny" Wyatt

"Never write a check in a liquor store."
—Jan Gentry

"There is no such thing as an unloaded gun"
when children are around."
—Jan Gentry

"The sheriff and the deputies are your children's friends; your children need to know they can come to us for help."
—Jan Gentry

"If it's good, there's no need to talk about it."
—Prince Parrish

"When you have someone die from a tragedy, you can't get everybody into the church; but when you have some old saint die of natural causes, you have to hire the pallbearers."
—Jan Gentry

"A Living Legend"

FEW EVER REACH THE STATUS OF A LEGEND. SHERIFF L.L. WYATT was legendary, bigger than life. Anyone who has ever heard of the man shakes their head in awe; he was something else. Fearless, courageous, fair, honest, in control of himself. He was a legend during his lifetime, a *living* legend. Today, he is still a legend. There are those to this day who swear they can still hear him jingling that change or tapping his fingers on that table in the courthouse. For years after Wyatt's death, some deputies would not go to the courthouse at night because they just knew Wyatt still stalked the halls.

For most, though, a man who believed that the law was our friend and enforced it fairly, a man whose personal life was above reproach, a man whose work carried a sense of calling from God, a man who listened to you, and a man who kept you safe at the risk of his own life, has to live on. No way can that man die. Even those who only read about Wyatt will not want to let him die as a role model.

Just ask the people of Greene County. Go visit the museum that has been established in Wyatt's memory. Housed in the administration building of the sheriff's headquarters, the memorabilia is guarded by deputies who are pleased to brag about the man in whose shadow they proudly live and work. Or drop by *The Herald Journal* and chat with Carey Williams, editor, or Jan Gentry Foster, reporter. Pop into the Greensboro Florist and listen to Joel McCray, county historian. Or stop in most any place in Greensboro and listen to stories of the man, L.L. Wyatt. Even when these folks are gone, talk to anyone who has lived in Greensboro long, and you will find the legend of Sheriff Loy Lee Wyatt still lives.

And just maybe you will be inspired to incorporate Wyatt's virtues into your everyday life and change your world.

Wyatt Plaque at the Jail Dedicated to His Memory

Sonny Wyatt Speaks at the Dedication of the Jail to Wyatt

Discussion Questions

1. Could Wyatt walk into situations today and get control? Would he be shot? Would he have to carry a gun?

2. Could a police officer or sheriff be "as honest as the day is long" today? How would that manifest itself?

3. What would Wyatt have to do today to gain the trust of a diverse community?

4. What would Wyatt be able to do today to cut through the perception of racism? How would he show that all lives matter?

5. How could Wyatt be a community police officer in today's culture? Could he do it in a big city? What would that look like?

6. What could someone like Wyatt contribute to young men in a city of drugs and crimes?

7. If you are in law enforcement, how is Wyatt a role model for you?

8. How is Wyatt a role model for young adults today struggling to find

a sense of calling or purpose in their occupation or profession? How does Wyatt show you that you can re-make your world?

9. How does Wyatt challenge you today?

10. In what ways can Wyatt be a hero for your children to emulate? What in Wyatt would you not want your children to emulate?

11. How does this story teach all people to be color-blind?

Sources

CREDIT FOR DIRECT PRINTED QUOTES

Introduction

"shot at, bitten, threatened…": Prentice Palmer, "Honesty is the First Requirement" (Augusta, Georgia: The Augusta Chronicle, 1969, September 23), p 3.

"you know the story…": Celestine Sibley, *Touch of the Shepherd* (Atlanta, Georgia: North Avenue Presbyterian Church, 1994), p. iii, Foreword.

"the more it seemed…": Ibid, p. iv, Foreword.

Chapter 1

"Hooch" and "shine"…": Jan Whyllson, *The Little Place That Almost Was* (Greensboro, Georgia: Rosemound and Oconee Associates, McCommons Desktop Publishing, etc., 2012), p. 33.

"cotton had been king…": John Companiotte, *Lingerlonger: A History of Reynolds Plantation*, (Greensboro, Georgia: The Lingerlonger Development Co., Third Edition, 2006), p. 20.

"They souped up their cars…": Rick Houston, "NASCAR'S Earliest Days Forever Connected to Bootlegging," (www.NASCAR.com/en-us/news-media/articles, 2012/11/moonshinemystique.html), Nov. 1.

"NASCAR'S Roots are Dipped...": Ibid.

Chapter 3

"I mean they had 12 to 15 vats...": Prentice Palmer. Ibid.
"You know I had a dream...": In Memory of The High Sheriff of
    Greene (Greensboro, Georgia: The Herald Journal, 2012, April 5),
    p. 22.
"The first sixty days...": Prentice Palmer, Ibid.

Chapter 5

"shot at; bitten; and cursed...": Ibid.
"stay out of the woods...": Ibid.
"that set me back...": Ibid.
"the next thing they tried": Ibid.
"I wish there had been a...": Ibid.
"Okay, Mr. Wyatt...": "County Policeman Wyatt Kills John Neal in
    Struggle" (Greensboro, Georgia: The Herald Journal, 1927, March
    11) n .p.
"My partner went down...": Keeler McCartney, "His Duels Are
    Legend" (Atlanta, Georgia: The Atlanta Constitution, October 15,
    1975), p. 15.
"the only reason he didn't shoot...": Prentice Palmer. Ibid.
"I took the Chief of Police...": Frank Ranew, Jr., "Greene sheriff eyes
    fall bid due to 'long-standing welcome'" (Augusta, Georgia: The
    Augusta Chronicle, 1972, March 21), p. 5. Source: GenealogyBank.
    com. Another source quotes Wyatt as saying he took the wounded
    officers to an ambulance which is perhaps more accurate since there
    was no hospital in Greensboro at the time. This quote is used for its
    description of the overall situation.

"I went over the...": Keeler McCartney. Ibid.

"I finally got a finger in his...": Ibid.

"The car chugged...": Ranew, Jr. Ibid.

"Tom, last night you...": Corey Crouse; Susan Enlandson; Tamie Moran; and Cynthia Smith, *Do Tell* (Greensboro, Georgia: Street Strategy. 2009), p. 51.

"Back in those days...": "Hollywood Writer to Write Book" (Greensboro, Georgia: The Herald Journal, 1975, November 28), p.1.

Chapter 7

"There's never been a hint...": Prentice Palmer: Ibid.

Chapter 8

"He was a religious man...": *Citation* (Greensboro, Georgia: Plaque at The 1859 Greensboro Jail).

Chapter 9

"I have someone to...": "A Tribute to Sheriff Wyatt" (Greensboro, Georgia: The Herald Journal, 1977, April 15), p. 1.

"I'm sorry I want to...": Ibid.

Chapter 12

"Is it true...": Bernice McCullar: "Greensboro's Most Famous Unknown Man" (Greensboro, Georgia: The Herald-Journal, 1999, March) Southland Jubilee ed.: 1

"No, sir...": Ibid.

Chapter 13

"I feel you will go down…": Cutline, photo of Wyatt and Nunn (Greensboro, Georgia: The Herald Journal, 1976, May), p. 13.

Chapter 14

"The first man I voted for was Wyatt…": Cutline, photo of Emma Davis (Greensboro, Georgia: The Herald Journal, n. d.), n.p.

"…four Negroes began school…": (Seattle, Washington: Seattle Daily Times, 1965, 11/17), p.20.

Chapter 16

"I tell my deputies…": Frank Ranew, Jr, Ibid.

"The man who gave me this…": "Executive of Bank Slain" (Brownsville, Texas: The Brownsville Herald, 1975, December 16), n. p.

"He was a mighty fine man…": "Banker Killed: Bizarre Robbery Brings Arrest" (High Point, North Carolina: The High Point Enterprise, 1975, December 16), n.p.

"Officers who went to Flynt's home…": Ibid.

Chapter 18

There are multiple accounts of how this event came down. To get as accurate a story as possible, I have consulted 12 different newspapers' accounts of this event and listened to the versions given in oral interviews. It is the one story told by almost everyone I interviewed. Throughout the year and a half of my writing, I continued to find new pieces to expand or to correct the story. I spent hours on this one chapter and in the process, learned how press deadlines and headlines affect a story. I also felt the pride in the local lore that keeps the drama alive and the sheriff a legend. Below are sources for printed quotes in the story.

"Drop back…": Associated Press, "Wild Chase in Georgia ends in death of alleged robber" (Mobile, Alabama: Mobile Register, 1974, December 19), p. 10.

"Let Us Through…": Associated Press, "Teller, Sheriff Tell of Shootout With Robbers" (Greenwood, South Carolina: The Index-Journal, 1974, December 20), p. 17.

"He was right on him…": Associated Press, "Wild Chase in Georgia…" Ibid.

"Ms. Eugenia Braswell was driving…": Ibid.

"Going through my head was…": Sam Hopkins, "'I Knew I Was Going to Die'" (Atlanta, Georgia: The Atlanta Journal, 1974, December 27), n.p.

"Don't shoot…": Associated Press, "Wild Chase in Georgia": Ibid.

"As soon as I had a chance, I fired…": Associated Press, "Third Robbery Suspect Arrested" (High Point, North Carolina: The High Point Enterprise, 1974, December 19), p. 1.

"I kept walking…": Associated Press, "Teller, Sheriff Tell of Shootout…": Ibid.

"He turned for an instant…": "A Legend In His Own Time" (Greensboro, Georgia: The Herald Journal, 1977, April 15), p. 1.

"this gun could have…": Keeler McCartney, "Sheriff Wyatt Lives 'On Borrowed Time'" (Atlanta, Georgia: The Atlanta Constitution, 1974, December 27), n.p.

"I Knew I Was Going to Go…": Sam Hopkins, 'I Knew I Was Going to Die,' Ibid.

"I Knew We Weren't Going…": Tom Harrison, "Defendant Admits to Bank Robbery" (Augusta, Georgia: Augusta Chronicle, 1975, August 20), p. 12.

"It's your job…": McCartney, Keeler. "Sheriff Wyatt Lives on Borrowed Time": Ibid.

"You don't think of being afraid…": Ibid.

"We hate to see anyone killed…": Ibid.

"I'm living on borrowed time…": Ibid.

"He is very quiet…": "Sheriff L.L. Wyatt Given Award" (Greensboro, Georgia: The Herald Journal, 1968, 9/27), p. 1.

Chapter 19

"People today are more law…": "Hollywood Writer to Write Book on Greene County Sheriff L.L. Wyatt". Ibid.

Chapter 20

"Today we bury a living legend…": *A Tribute to Sheriff Wyatt* (Greensboro, GA: The Herald Journal, 1977, April 15), p. 1.

"He represented…": Sam Nunn, Senator. Letter of Condolence. (Greensboro, GA: Wyatt Museum).

"Sheriff Wyatt was loved…": George Busbee, Governor of Georgia. Letter of Condolence. (Greensboro, GA: Wyatt Museum).

Chapter 23

"Wyatt's own words on law enforcement…": Prentice Palmer. "Honesty is the First Requirement." Ibid. and Ranew, Frank, Jr. "Greene sheriff eyes fall bid due to 'long-standing welcome.'" Ibid.

"I believe I am a public servant…": Billy Hobbs. "Donnie Harrison Takes Over… Replaces Longtime Sheriff Chris Houston." Ibid., The Herald Journal, 2016, January 28), p.13.

Credits for Visuals

Unknown. Photographs. Greensboro, GA. Sonny and Madeleine Wyatt. Wyatt Family Archive. Used with permission.

"Sonny Wyatt at Three Years."

"Wyatt as Young Man."

"Wyatt on Patrol."

"Estelle as Young Woman."

"Wyatt with Sonny."

"Miss Estelle with Sonny as a Baby."

"Wyatt with Sonny at ten years of age."

"There is no substitute for experience" Campaign Poster

"Wyatt Watches to see Who is Buying Large Bags of Sugar."

"Re-elect Wyatt." Campaign Poster.

"Sheriff and Mrs. Wyatt at Home."

"Sonny Speaks at Dedication of 1895 Jail to Wyatt's Memory."

"Sonny and Madeleine Wedding in Cimmaron, New Mexico."

United States Army. "Sonny Promoted to Colonel." Photograph. Sonny Wyatt and Madeleine Wyatt. Wyatt Family Archive. Used with permission.

L.L. Wyatt. "Letter to Parole Board." Greensboro, GA. Scan of Letter. Sonny and Madeleine Wyatt. Wyatt Family Archive, Greensboro, GA. Used with permission.

Stancill, Lee. Greensboro, GA. Photographs of Memorabilia, The Wyatt Museum. 2016. Used with permission.

Senator Sam Nunn. "Letter to Estelle Wyatt."

Governor Carl Sanders. "Letter to L.L. Wyatt."

Governor George Busbee. "Letter to Estelle Wyatt."

"The Guns and The Headlines of Wyatt's Heroics in Wren's Bank Robbery"

"Giant Liquor Still Raided"

Stancill, Lee. Greensboro, GA. Greene County Sheriff's Office Gallery.
Personal Collection. Used with permission.
"The Greene County 1895 Jail."
"Friends Honor Wyatt."
Hertzler, Claire Underwood. Photographs. Greensboro, GA. Personal
Collection. 2016.
"Plaque Dedicating the 1895 Jail to Memory of L. L. Wyatt."
"One of the Oldest Courthouses in Georgia."
"The Roll-Top Desk Wyatt Used in Courthouse."
Hertzler, Claire Underwood. Greensboro, GA. Photograph of Wyatt
Memorabilia, The Wyatt Museum. 2016.
"Name Plate for Wyatt's new home on S East Street."
The Herald Journal. Greensboro, GA. News Stories and Photographs.
Used with permission.
"Watering the Ground With Mash Was a Frequent Happening
with Wyatt."
"Judge Brown Swears Wyatt In 1973."
"The Sheriff and the Senator."
"Mrs. Emma Davis at 103 Years of Age Votes for Wyatt."
"Whiskey Still Caught."
"Wyatt Investigates Crime Scene with Georgia Crime Bureau."
Bruso, Emily. Atlanta, GA. Emily B Photography. Photograph. "Author
Head Shot." August, 2016.

Oral Interview Acknowledgements:

Wyatt, Lloyd Lee. Oral History Interviews, January - July 2015.
Wyatt, Madeleine, Oral History Interviews, January –December 2015;
January—May 2016.
Wyatt, Andy, Oral History Phone Interview, May 2015.

McCray, Joel. Oral History Interview, February, June 2015; February 2016.

Boswell, L. G. Oral History Interview, March 2015.

Boswell, Linda. Oral History Interview, March 2015.

Voyles, Robert. Oral History Interview, April 2015.

Voyles, Caroline. Oral History Interview, April 2015, May 2016.

Tolbert, Comer. Oral History Interview, May 2015.

Parrish, Prince. Oral History Interview, August 2015.

Parrish, Scott. Oral History Phone Interview, July 2015.

Williams, Carey, Jr. Oral History Interviews, January 2015 — May 2016.

Foster, Jan Gentry. Oral History Interviews, January 2015 - May 2016.

Marchman, Ray. Oral History Interview, February 2015, March 2016.

Underwood, W. Perry. Oral History Interview, February 2015, March, May 2016.

Stone, W. L. "Pep." Oral History Interview, February 2016.

Callaway, Reed. Oral History Interview, September 2015, May 2016.

Dowdy, Alvin. Oral History Phone Interview, August 2015.

Jacobs, Nancy Webb. Oral History Phone Interview, February 2015, June 2016.

Webb, Roger. Oral History Interview, February 2015.

Chapman, Carolyn. Oral History Interview, February 2015.

Ogletree, Laverne. Oral History Interview, March 2015.

McCommons, Steve. Oral History Interview, March 2015.

Rhodes, C. L. "Mutt", Jr. Oral History Interview, May 2015.

Rhodes, Jane Chandler. Oral History Interview, May 2015.

Sarden, Eddie. Oral History Phone Interview, March 2016.

McKinley, Nettie. Oral History Interview, August 2015.

Jackson, Nancy. Oral History Interview, June 2015.

Duvall, Lewis. Oral History Interview, February 2015.

Peek, Jason. Oral History Phone Interview, September 2015.

Foster, Vivian. Oral History Interview, March 2016.

Foster, Shirley. Oral History Interview, March 2016, June 2016.

Moon, Richard. Oral History Phone Interview, April 2016.

Cathy, Joanne Newsome. Oral History Phone Interview, May, June 2016.

Moore, Everett. Oral History Interview, August 2015.

Askew, Allen, Oral Phone Interview, June 2016.

Bibliography

"The Famous Unknown Man." Greensboro, Georgia: *The Herald Journal*, March 1999, Southland Jubilee ed.:1.

Rice, T. B. and Williams, C.W. *History of Greene County Georgia*. Macon, Georgia: J.W. Burke Co., 1961.

Whyllson, Jan, *The Little Place That Almost Was*. Greensboro, Georgia: Rosemound and Oconee Associates, McCommons Desktop Publishing, etc., 2012.

Campaniotte, John, *Lingerlonger: A History of Reynolds Plantation*. Greensboro, Georgia: The Lingerlonger Development Company, Third Edition, 2006.

Crouse, Corey; Enlandson, Susan; Moragan, Tamie; and Smith, Cynthia, *Do Tell*. Greensboro, Georgia: Street Strategy, 2009.

The Greene County Heritage Book Committee, *Greene County, Georgia, Heritage 1786 — 2009*. Greensboro, Georgia: 2009.

Manthorne, Jason. "Greensboro." New Georgia Enclopedia.01 February 2016.Web.14 June 2016.

Acknowledgements

TO EACH OF YOU WHO ENCOURAGED ME IN ANY WAY ALONG THE way, I say thanks. And as the list grew longer and longer, I cherished each of you still. You deserve to be acknowledged.

My thanks go first to my dear Prayer Group friends, Mary Renshaw, Sharon Bailey, and Judy Holzman, who exclaimed, "Claire, there's your book!" and then cheered and prayed me through the hurdles, making my journey seem divinely seamless.

I am indebted to the Wyatt family, Lloyd Lee "Sonny", and Madeleine, for the hours we spent together at their home on Lake Oconee, remembering, recording, and reviewing photos and documents. Without their sustained interest and encouragement, I doubt the book would have happened. Their welcoming me into the family archives and their embracing me as the author has kept me on task. Thanks to their oldest son, Andy, for his impressions of his grandfather. I really tried to have this done for Sonny!

I am most grateful to Lloyd T. Whitaker, Founder and President of the Newleaf Corporation in Smyrna, Georgia, for his Endorsement. Lloyd grew up in Greene County (his mother was my history teacher), so he knew the Sheriff personally and the lore following him.

I owe bushels to Carey Williams, Editor, *The Herald Journal*, Greensboro, who is a walking archive of anything Greensboro and Georgia and a close friend of Wyatt. On most of the more than 25 trips to Greene County, I dropped into the newspaper office unannounced. Carey was always available to chat, to tell more stories or give more details and referrals. He is a master storyteller and could have done the book so well himself but elected to encourage me. And thanks to Jan Foster, reporter, for stopping her work to chat so many times about her years of working as Wyatt's administrative assistant.

Many, many thanks to Joel McCray, Greensboro Florist, and Chair of the Greene County Historical Society for also letting me pop in to chat, to get referrals, and to garner his stories and impressions. He is the epitome of a Southern storyteller, both in voice and in vocabulary.

My particular thanks go to Wyatt family friend, Dale Page, for his literary feedback and for his generosity in allowing me access to his unpublished research from Wyatt family records and other sources.

Many thanks go to Barbara Latta for her editing expertise freely given.

Thanks, to my Underwood siblings, Carroll, John, Lowell, Gilbert, Weyman, Perry, and Lanelle U. LaRue for their encouragement and belief in me. Special thanks to Lanelle for getting each of us a copy of *The Greensboro Heritage Book of 2009*, where I got my first glimpse of Wyatt and his national fame. And to Perry, for hosting me overnight at his home in Greensboro, for his stories, for his reviewing the copy, and for the lunches he often bought me. Thanks to nieces Beverly U. Hurndon and Lynn U. Mosley for their helpful critique.

My appreciation goes, too, to Sherri Oxendine, my hairstylist, for connecting me with the Foster sisters and her co-worker and writer, Greg Dobraz, for his expertise and encouragement. And to Sharon, Judy, Mary, and neighbor Shelley Thompson for their getting me unstuck from the first chapter.

Thanks to you who offered time for oral interviews in person or via phone. You gave action to the book, and the thirty-five of you are listed under Oral Interviews. And to Betty Moncrief Eley and Jason Peek for bequeathing me clippings of Wyatt stories they had not been able to part with before.

The biggest bear hug I can give and praise beyond measure go to Eugene M. Hertzler, my husband, and the lifter of my arms when I was tired. His prayers have kept me focused on my calling. He has eagerly listened to each new story, eating them for dinner each time I returned from Greensboro. As I neared the finish line, Gene ate off Wyatt place mats as the book was spread over the dining room table for months. He is a love. I am blessed. And thanks to daughter and son-in-law Megan and Aaron Gebauer-Hertzler for their interest and backing all along the way, from the West Coast.

Thanks to the Sunday at 10 Prayer group at North Ave. Presbyterian Church, particularly Emily and Adam Bruso, for lifting me up during this process of writing and seeing me as the one to write it. Now you can pray for sales!

And I am extremely grateful to Bob Babcock at Deeds Publishing for affirming the Wyatt story so quickly and for his attentiveness and that of his staff throughout the publishing process. Deeds was my first choice after a lengthy interaction with Bob and his staff at the Decatur Book Festival in 2015. They have been an author's dream publisher.

In addition to the people, I am grateful for the many coffee shops and libraries where writers can hang out. Two places, in particular, were my go-to sanctuaries. Early in the writing, I would drive forty minutes to the Monastery of the Holy Spirit in Conyers and spend the day in their Wi-Fi café, writing undisturbed. And perusing the gift shop or joining the monks for prayers to break up the day. Then, just as I needed to maximize my time the most, I discovered access to the John Bulow Campbell Library at Columbia Presbyterian Seminary, just five minutes from my house in Decatur! It was usually as much of a haven as the monastery and a place I could go for shorter periods. The staff there deserves acknowledgment for their kind and ever-ready assistance.

The writer's clubs have my acknowledgment, too: The East Metro Atlanta Christian Writer's group in Covington, the Scribblers in Norcross, and the Greensboro Writer's Guild. Each group was ever encouraging even though I could not attend regularly. The Atlanta Writer's Club was the venue through which I first met Bob and Jan Babcock and learned of Deeds Publishing. I cannot say enough about the Decatur Book Festival, to which I walked each Labor Day weekend for ten years and drank in every ounce of wisdom from the "biggies." Writers need writers and the Decatur Book Festival is one of the best venues.

About the Author

THOUGH THIS IS HER FIRST BOOK, CLAIRE UNDERWOOD HERTZLER is uniquely qualified to write *The High Sheriff of Greene* as she grew up in the Wyatt culture of Greene County, GA. "There go Wyatt and Taylor," she remembers hearing as the sheriff whizzed by in a cloud of dust with his deputy. Claire has written the story of this legendary sheriff from over 30 oral interviews and countless newspaper accounts. She has brought Wyatt alive again to those who knew him and for those who wished they had. In this little gem of a book, Claire Hertzler has preserved a slice of Georgia history sure to captivate and inspire.

Claire's blog, www.justclairefying.wordpress.com, deals with current issues, observations about living, and profiles of folks inspiring others.

Her writings include these published articles: "Travel Insurance Tips," *Transitions Abroad Magazine,* "Encounter With God," *Church Recreation Magazine,* and "Easter at Flat Rock," *Georgia Magazine,* also about history in Greene County, Georgia. She has had two articles accepted for *Fruits of the Spirit,* an anthology being edited by the East Metro Atlanta Christian Writers.

In addition to writing, Claire enjoys cooking, gardening, fashion, and travel. She holds degrees from Mercer University, Southwestern Seminary, and GA State University. She has professional experience in the fields of public education, Christian education, volunteer services administration, and non-profits. She was one of the first activists fighting human trafficking in Atlanta, an interest she maintains. She is active in the North Avenue Presbyterian Church in Atlanta.

Claire enjoys living in Decatur, GA with her husband, Eugene. She especially enjoys the mornings they treat themselves to a cappuccino at one of the many coffee shops in Decatur. And she is a regular at the Decatur Book Festival.

CPSIA information can be obtained at www.ICGtesting.com
Printed in the USA
LVOW07s0300051016

507245LV00004B/6/P